Noticing the Constant

Offer of God

Noticing the Constant Offer of God

Randy Mark Williams

with illustrations by
Meaghan Iversen

Gabriel & Ives Editions
Burnaby, Canada

Gabriel & Ives Editions
9154 Saturna Drive, Suite 101
Burnaby, British Columbia V3J 7K2
Email inquiries: gieditions@telus.net

Copyright ©2021 by Randy Mark Williams
www.randywilliams.ca

Cover design and illustrations ©2021 by Meaghan Iversen

First Edition: January 2021

ISBN-13: 978-1-7771-7872-7

For Messrs. Gabriel and Ives, who have endured more stories, puns, and viewings of *Yellow Submarine* than lesser men could bear.

Contents

Acknowledgements

Many thanks to the fine folk who cajoled and supported me throughout this book's creation. There are a particular few that I would like to single out for duty above and beyond comprehension. Meaghan Iversen, a conjurer of painstakingly complex line drawings, brilliantly responded to my request to contribute illustrations with "as few lines as possible." The fastidious proofreading of Norma J. Hill has (again) ably steered me clear of grammatical *faux pas* and critical guffaws. A tip o' the hat is gratefully extended to Rev. Dr. Jason Byassee, who suggested writing a book in a manner that made it seem like a perfectly sane idea. Evidently sanity is in the eye of the beholder. Above all, this book is a reality because of the outrageously generous support of my wife, Marilyn. Thank you for the hours spent reading, the months spent encouraging, and the years spent inspiring. With you, "I am the happiest creature in the world."

Part One

Noticing

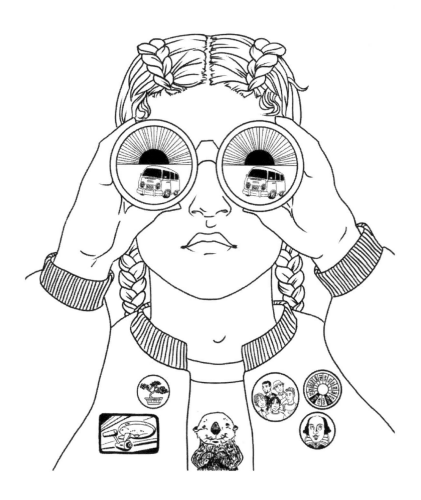

Introduction

Do you ever catch yourself talking back to a book? I sure hope so, because the book you are holding is quite chatty. Sure, it's a theological book, but growing up it always wanted to be a conversation. This is a book that doesn't want paper and ink to get in the way of a good chin wag, unexpected stories, or out-and-out heartwarming foolishness. Consider yourself warned: this book is an invitation to partake of a journey that may induce muttering, snickering, thinking, and a whole lot of noticing. Yes, noticing – whatever that may mean – is top of our agenda.

This book's alter ego is a previously published monograph with the staid title, *Graced Existence: Grace and Experience in the Theology of Karl Rahner*. The three years of research behind *Graced Existence* alerted me to an inescapable and lamentable fact: books by, and about, the Jesuit theologian Karl Rahner, aren't very amusing. Truth be told, they almost never have funny drawings. *Noticing the Constant Offer of God* is, in part, my attempt to address these oversights. In the following pages you will encounter stories in which noticing, God, and Rahner's grace-fueled insights gleefully collide with my life. You'll also encounter input from a host of well-known and little-known Christian thinkers … and maybe even bump into H.G. Wells, Sherlock Holmes, Scooby-Doo, a feuding boyband, and a little town in Idaho along the way. Make no mistake, noticing covers a lot of ground. So, are you in? You, and as many friends as we can fit in the NUV, are cordially invited to cover some noticing ground. NUV? Don't worry, you'll notice this makes sense soon enough.

As might be expected, any book that can be loosely classified as "mirthfully introspective" is bound to have a bit of a split personality. The book you're now perusing is no exception. In the first half, noticing is introduced and held up to the light for a proper inspection: Just what exactly is *Noticing the Constant Offer of God?* The second half is where the theological cows come home. It wrestles the lessons learned up front into something that sneakily resembles practical application. The two halves together conspire to introduce a (soon to be) popular adage: *Noticing is serious business, but noticing that you've noticed is where the life-changing action is.* Once again, are you in? Are you willing to have a conversation with a book? Excellent! I'll meet you at the beginning of chapter one. Let the noticing begin!

R.M.W.
October 2020

1

My Story
(or When I Noticed … and Noticed that I Noticed)

L et me start with a confession: I am not one of *those* high-profile noticing experts. Sure, their sage is all the rage, but we're not going to be jumping onto *that* bandwagon. That's right, there's a certain something we need to get straight right here at the starting line: Noticing is *not* mindfulness. In recent years there has been a big push to make us all mindful of mindfulness. Mindfulness has become big business. There are high profile mindfulness gurus, and they're influencing everything from educational institutions to navel-gazing self-improvement talk shows. These gurus turn up on our bookstore shelves and on our glowing blogosphere screens. Mind you, I don't really mind them. It just seems best that you know I'm not one of them. I don't want you to drag along everything you've read or heard about mindfulness on our noticing journey. That's right, we're going on a journey. We're breaking out and noticing on our own. If it helps you can call it *noticefulness*, although I promise I won't.

One of the peculiarities of this book is that it puts a lot of weight on the word "notice." Merriam-Webster might even sneer at some of the ways I see fit to stretch this word. Whatever shape it takes, noticing is always an encounter. Noticing alerts us. Whether we pay attention is another matter. It's a well-known fact that our everyday lives are bombarded with things vying for our attention. Today, we're all targets. I suspect that if there truly was anything simpler about bygone horse-drawn eras, it probably has something to do with their lack of snow tire ads. Not long ago I read an article on *Forbes.com* estimating that most Americans are exposed to between 4,000 and 10,000 advertisements each day.[1] Even the low end is scary. With that kind of onslaught, it's no wonder that noticing can be a largely unconscious affair. We often don't pay close attention to what our eyes and ears notice. If we took it all in, our heads would explode.

It seems to me that all of the corporate logos and social media burps hurled our way each day are like unwanted fingerprints. They leave residue marks all over the furniture of our lives. Just as soon as we scrub them off, more prints and smudgy smears appear. But not all fingerprints are bad. There are folks who look at a rose garden and see the fingerprints of God. It isn't uncommon for natural beauty to be celebrated as God's mark, or fingerprint, on the world. I will say, and will say quite often, that such fingerprints are actually *pointers*. The flowers themselves are not God's presence on earth, but rather, are a presence that points to God. They are *signposts* that guide our attention. When we look at a rose garden, we have an opportunity to notice the flowers as signposts that point beyond their physical leaves and blooms.

Our noticing journey wouldn't take us too far if beautiful roses were the first and last word on noticing God. A rose is just the nicely perfumed icing on the cake. I know this because in my personal story it's the whole cake that smells ... you might say it stinks to high heaven. That the book you're reading exists at all is on account of my personal rose-free story. Strap yourself in. In travel jargon, this story is our departure gate for points unnoticed. It is an absolutely true account of the moment that I noticed myself noticing the constant offer of God. I'll start with the big bang idea and then sort through the particles that it projects at us.

BANG: EVERYTHING POINTS TO GOD.

A dozen years after my smelly awakening, I'm still sorting through the cosmic debris this big bang unearthed (can you say "unearthed" when talking about a cosmic mind melt?). Everything points to God. This is not a new thought by any means, but it is a thought that has to be noticed before it is accepted as reality. It is much more than a statement. It's a declaration on the dynamics of the reality in which we *all* live. That makes it a universal statement. It isn't something that can be true for just some *special* people. Either everything points to God or it doesn't. So here is my case, based on my ongoing unravelling of a life-changing event.

In the Milky Way Galaxy, on the planet Earth, on the west coast of Canada, in the suburbs of Vancouver, one back lane west of the crossroads of Austin Avenue and Schoolhouse Street, in a parking lot at 49⁰14'58.3"N latitude and 122⁰51'19.2"W longitude, I looked at a garbage bin ... and noticed for the first time in my life, that garbage bins are references to God.

This is what I noticed:

The garbage bin was the large commercial kind. It was one of those big metal boxes with a hinged lid. Noticing the bin, it dawned on me that metals are extracted from geological materials – things that are derived from the earth. No God – No Earth – No garbage bins. But there are garbage bins! With this I noticed that the earth, and the entire cosmos, are visible reference points in our lives which point to God. When I notice them, I am noticing material references to God.

The garbage bin was fabricated with intention. Human minds creatively used human intellectual gifts to adapt the metal for a specific use. I noticed that the garbage bin existed as a visible reference to the invisible intellectual capacity gifted to humankind. Therefore, all cognitive activity exists in reference to God. All thought occurs and is expressed by God-given intellectual capabilities manifest in human physicality – our bodies. Along with the material reference, I noticed a cognitive reference.

The garbage bin smelled noticeably like burnt gym socks with a side of forgotten eggs. It was located in the parking lot of the church where I was serving on the pastoral staff. The bin's cargo was a heady mix of the weekly vacuum dust and after-service food leftovers that constitutes the average suburban church trash. Even in bins adjacent to a house of worship, coffee grounds and stale lemon squares don't improve with age. But that smell! That smell was a jarring olfactory experience pointing my senses to the material garbage in the intelligently fabricated garbage bin. I guess that made it a material reference/cognitive reference mash-up. My stinky sensory experience – like *all* sensory experience – ultimately points to God.

Eureka! This bang revealed to me that I can't see a garbage bin, or recognize the use of a garbage bin, without reference to God. This is a heck of a reality to notice: Everything points to God. I can't think of a thought or see an object without it pointing towards God. All that is material and immaterial points beyond itself. I can't see any *thing* or have any *thought* without it participating in a relation to God.

The immensity of this takes some time to settle in. It is the reality we have all lived with up to the moment you are reading this. Yet, owning it as *our* reality – that the totality of life is lived in relation to God – takes some sorting through. There are some far-reaching issues to investigate here. While working through them, let's remember to stay mindful of my earlier statement that this is a *universal* reality. That's right, I'm

Eureka!

going to allow mindfulness to encroach just this once. It is key that our shared situation is a universal reality. We can't opt in or opt out of it. What we do, rather, is notice it to differing degrees. I'll come back to this. The important point now is that we're all in on this. We all have the same pointers that trigger our noticing. God doesn't play favourites here. To be human is to share a framework of existence we call life. All life is lived in relation to God.

Have I gone overboard with my universal statements? Let's ask around. Let's imagine that you and me, and all the people who have read the opening pages of this book, are gathered in a big room. Together we make a pretty diverse group. Picture our group happily chatting face-to-face, and me standing up and unequivocally announcing that "all life is lived in relation to God." I expect that such an emphatic claim would draw the attention of most of our happy chatterers. So, how would our group react? How would you react? Amongst our group I think some folks would simply agree. Their minds connect the ideas that God is *the* Creator and all creation is related to God. Even so, other folks might fuss a bit. They might see God as Creator of *things*, yet balk at the idea that "all" – not just every *thing* – relates to God. Is a thought a thing? Is a smell a thing? We can wrap our hands around a bagel thing or a jewelry thing, but not an idea or a smell. Others in the room wouldn't even go so far as to accept *every* material thing in my statement. For some, it seems plausible that God is the cause of the cosmic big bang that launched the galaxies, but God's relationship with creation stops there. If that's the case, then the bagels we bake in the twenty-first century are pretty far removed from a direct relation to God.

God's presence and relationship to creation are massive issues. Naturally they generate a mass of questions that garner massively diverse responses among any large group. It's always been this way. Unlike our above-mentioned twenty-first century bagels, many important observations are spread out across history. And while it is certainly wise to only swallow the most current bagels, theological ideas are different. A diet comprised of only current ideas limits our engagement with timeless questions. The renowned British author C. S. Lewis (1898-1963) coined a name for our tendency to place a higher value on "new" ideas than on preceding ones. He called it *chronological snobbery*. Lewis defined chronological snobbery as "the uncritical acceptance of the intellectual climate common to our own age and the assumption that whatever has gone out of date is on that count discredited."[2] Whoa, that sounds pretty bad. Who would do that? Well, most of us do at one time or another. I'm not just talking about preferring current medical practices to medieval leech therapy. Consider this: does the idea of using the cell phone you purchased five years ago (when it was the "latest") sound scandalous? For some folks that model is five purchases old. Today it is, as Lewis said, "discredited." The same holds true for basketball sneakers. The entire sneaker industry is based on displacing yesterday's signature shoes with today's newer signature shoes. In the cell phone and sneaker industries, and in multiple other facets of everyday life, chronological snobbery rules.

This devotion to current thinking extends to fundamental ideas as well. At the turn of the millennium (when 20th century bagels magically became 21st century bagels), I worked for a business headquartered in picturesque Portland, Oregon. I was based in Canada and visited the Portland office every few months. One day I visited the office and discovered that one employee had introduced a new chair idea. Actually, it wasn't a chair in the traditional sense. It was an inflated ball made for sitting on; a new chair replacement. Apparently, this was the wave of the future. The next time I visited, the office had a dozen of these balls in use. The very next visit after that they had none. That is, they had none being used as chairs. The folks who bought them still kept them for a while, cluttering up their offices and cubicles. Maybe they were waiting for balancing on a ball to become as functional as a traditional chair. Maybe they were just too embarrassed to let go of the idea. Chronological snobbery and vanity are known to keep company.

I'm not sharing this *newest is bestest* story to highlight that the balancing chair balls point to God (but yeah, they do). I'm sharing it to highlight an important question: Do we want the wisdom of a fixed moment in time or do we want to seek out timeless wisdom? Let's face it, if you're set on building a functional chair, you need to study the time-honoured four-leg design. Similarly, our pursuit of insight into the notion that all life is lived in relation to God will definitely require input from across the ages. Following my garbage bin experience, I have kept my antennae up to hone in on important thinkers who have grappled with the questions of everyday human orientation to God. I'm going to bring some of them into our journey path from time to time, so that we might listen and learn from them. Some thinkers will be ancient and some will be recent. C. S. Lewis was a particularly good start. Lewis recognized the shortcomings of the chronological snobbery tendencies in his own life, and strove to overcome them.

Among the more recent brains that we'll be picking, you'll note my fondness for Karl Rahner (1904-1984). Rahner was an influential Jesuit theologian whose work has helped me explore how my garbage bin eureka and my faith connect. I'll quote him more than anyone else as we go along. When it comes to combating our chronological snobbery, Rahner provides us with a convenient meeting place between eras. His 20th century thinking is not so old that it seems foreign. Yet, in our age of blender-speed accelerating post-post-modern change, Rahner is ever-increasingly *not* current. Will our era allow his ideas to converse with us as we journey, or banish them to a storage room for yesterday's four-leg theological chairs?

The thought that a Christian would reject important theological contributions from past centuries should sound ridiculous. After all, none of the books that make up the Bible were written recently. Nor is the Bible you purchase today a new-and-improved model. The Bible is a source of ancient wisdom. The Church Fathers, theologians who helped the church navigate scripture in the early centuries following Jesus' revelatory life and death, also impart significant wisdom. This too should be a ridiculously obvious statement. Of course, it's only obvious after we spend some time with their written legacy. We have to make time to go to the Church Fathers because they are seldom brought to us. Christians in North America can hear a great many Sunday sermons before hearing a single reference to names like Ambrose, Athanasius, or Augustine (to name but a few from the tip of the Church Father alphabet).

The intellectual output of the theologians who precede us point to God. However, so does the intellectual output of today's thinkers in all fields, and the cognitive activity of that suspect kid who packs your bags at the grocery store. Yes, even him! The ideas of all humankind, including you and me, point to God in a myriad of ways. Sometimes these ideas are the thoughts and comments we share about God. Sometimes they are far removed from theological talk. Even the oddest things that enter our minds exist in a chain of references to God. The references relate in a way that is akin to the *six degrees of separation from Kevin Bacon* game. If you have pulled this book out of a time capsule, the game was a popular twentieth-century relationship game. One player offers up the name of a well-known person; often the name of a popular actor from another era. The opposing player then takes up the challenge of connecting that bygone actor to Kevin Bacon (another thespian, check out the copy of *Footloose* in the time capsule). Players are allowed up to six relationship connections (each is a "degree of separation") to move from the challenge name to Kevin Bacon. The fewer connections the better. If you're a trivia hound you might even impress your friends by connecting people across multiple eras. Here's an example:

BARBARA STANWYCK acted in *The Lady Eve* (1941) with HENRY FONDA

HENRY FONDA was in the movie *Fail-Safe* (1964) with WALTER MATHAU

WALTER MATHAU was in *Grumpy Old Men* (1993) with JACK LEMON

JACK LEMON was in *JFK* (1991) with TOMMY LEE JONES

TOMMY LEE JONES was in *No Country for Old Men* (2007) with JOSH BROLIN

JOSH BROLIN was in *Hollow Man* (2000) with **KEVIN BACON**.[3]

Violà! A Barbara Stanwyck to Kevin Bacon chain of reference that keeps within the six degrees of separation limit. That's pretty good.

The same principle works with any pointer's relation to God. In the next example God stands in for Kevin Bacon, and the challenge name is a random thought instead of an actor. For a random thought challenge word, I'll use BAGEL (why not, it worked before). Here goes:

BAGEL is made with FLOUR

FLOUR is ground-up WHEAT

WHEAT grows in EARTH

EARTH was created by **GOD**.

Only 4 degrees of separation for our bagel to point to God. Of course, I could have steered clear of the material references to God and stuck with the cognitive ones. Something like this:

BAGEL is a WORD

WORD exists in LANGUAGE

LANGUAGE is a product of INTELLECT

INTELLECT is a facet of HUMANITY

HUMANITY is made possible by **GOD**.

Aha! You can see how the last move could have been the first move: BAGEL is made possible by GOD. In this light, our bagel – like any and all bagels – points directly to God. Even the idea *bagel*, the human ingenuity to devise bagel, and the word bagel, point to God. If you're thinking that the degrees of separation game looks a lot like my garbage bin moment in slow motion, you are absolutely correct. The game is a frame-by-frame scan of what my brain did when the wisdom of the garbage bin hit me. It is yet another way of communicating our big bang idea: EVERYTHING POINTS TO GOD.

We have revisited this premise to ensure it is firm in our minds. It has to be clear, because talking about references to God will inevitably attract attention. Like all big bang ideas, pointers are a push-back target for those who challenge the notion of a Creator who has made all things possible. Ask anyone who has ever dared to mention the most obvious Easter subject matter at a community Easter dinner. Talking about God, whether you're in a wee phone booth or a massive crowd, is a tricky business. When we talk about God, we are sharing ideas and concepts that shape how we see God. Our ideas portray how we perceive God's character and authority and presence amongst us. Being human, we end up sharing decidedly human ideas. This brings us to an important question: what is stopping our idea of God from becoming a blank screen that we project *our* thoughts and wishes onto? The whole idea of noticing God becomes moot if all of our pointers are directed toward a drive-in movie screen in the sky.

Our very human intellect has the capacity to project human ideals and characteristics onto a grand God idea. This ability to fashion a made-to-order God is a legitimate and longstanding concern. In her book, *Bird by Bird*, Anne Lamott shares that "You can safely assume you've created God in your own image when it turns out that God hates all the same people you do." Lamott credits this insight to her friend Tom Weston, a Jesuit priest, and clearly, a keen student of human nature.[4] It's best to let God be God and focus on appreciating God as God is. Our part is to steer away from adapting the old cliché, *I don't know art but I know what I like.* Art is about preferences but God is not. *I don't know God but I know what I like* just doesn't work. Noticing is discovery, not construction.

Worries over imposing human ideals on divine deity are age old. Back before the Christian era, and even before Socrates, there was a Greek poet we know as Xenophanes of Colophon (ca. 560-470 BC). Xenophanes objected to the qualities and behaviours that Homer and Hesiod attributed to the gods. These are the gods that take center stage in the epic poems and stories of Greek mythology. The gods were being portrayed as figures who engaged in the same devious and illicit behaviours that were condemned in humans. Instead of exhibiting conduct that reflected genuine divine perfection, Xenophanes felt the gods were being depicted as little more than supercharged humans.

In the Christian sphere similar conflicts arise from time to time. In the 1840's the German philosopher Ludwig Feuerbach (1804-1872) caused a ruckus with his ideas about human nature and God. We could demonstrate his message by putting a mirror over the altar of your local church, along with a

Caution: Humans at Work sign on the church door. Looking up to the altar mirror, we would only see ourselves. Then, if we mistook this image for God, our understanding of the church's mission would be derived from human error, not divine wisdom. In other words: we'd be in an alarming fix because our inward human nature was being outwardly projected onto a faulty idea of God. Picturing Feuerbach's speculation in this way, we can see the chief consequence of accepting his theory. It requires reducing our perception of God to an idealized reflection of humanity.

Feuerbach's conclusions reflect his very generous assessment of human nature. He saw human intellect, will, and feeling as perfections of our species. In his view the potential of each perfection is essentially limitless. There are some twists and turns to his thinking, but the outcome is this: When the attributes of our entire species are looked upon as an object, that object is seen to exist outside of each individual person. In this divide, it is this separate unlimited object (of human perfections) that we see as God. In this way, Feuerbach suggests that the attributes we associate with God's perfect character and eternal authority are simply a projected amalgam of human ideals.

That's enough of the heavy stuff for now. I have raised the concerns of Xenophanes and Feuerbach for a darn good reason. I want to acknowledge them and then dismiss them. That's right, I invited them in just to show them the door (the door, of course, points to God). Xenophanes and Feuerbach bring up good issues … but they are *not* noticing issues. Sure, we'll be working with pointers that are signpost towards God, but God won't need to duck. These pointers don't project anything *at* God. They don't add, they don't take away, they simply prompt us to notice. So, if you have human-projection pointing concerns in mind as we approach the idea of noticing God, let's put them aside now. Our concern is not with constructing a humanly understood idea of God. We will be working with the premise that when we engage with God, we are engaging divine mystery. *Divine mystery* is a reality that declares *God doesn't look like us.* True, we may never understand why Michael Jackson chose to wear just one glove. But in the grand scheme of things humans aren't *that* mysterious – not divinely mysterious – not even that suspect kid who packs your groceries. If we keep this truth in mind, we don't have to worry about ending up with a God who looks like us. We can simply keep our eyes (and hearts) open to real-time notice the constant offer of God. Friends, its *auf wiedersehen, sayonara,* and *buenos noches* to Xenophanes and Feuerbach. We're leaving them behind; we have some noticing to do.

The task of this opening chapter has been twofold. Aside from setting a world record for using the word *bagel* in a theological setting (17 times!), I also wanted to share my story. At the end of the day, and throughout the day for that matter, noticing has a personal place in my life. Of course, this opening gambit also provided a swell opportunity to mention some theological thinkers, Kevin Bacon, and even that suspect kid (you know the one). If at this point you've made the acquaintance of a material thing, a thought thing, and a sensory-experience thing, then our journey is underway. The garbage bin, the design of the bin, and the smell of the garbage are pointer examples that are close to my heart. You can, of course, substitute your own material, cognitive and experiential stuff as you please. My garbage is there for you, but I don't mind if you use your own hat rack, back pack, or pet rat to cement the point. What's important is that we're not limiting the scope of the pointers we envision as signposts referencing God.

It's time to move on. There are details to sort through. The biggest is unravelling the title of this book: Just what is the "constant offer of God?" We're going to get there, but for starters we have three types of pointers to deal with.

2

Pointers to God

(the Visible and the Invisible)

If you routinely while away the hours picking through government documents on the National Aeronautics and Space Administration website, you might already know the following financial fun fact. However, there is an outside chance that not everyone (with a life) engages in space snooping audits. This then, is for the benefit of those who have escaped the gravitational pull of NASA online. After all, informational space debris, like all space junk, belongs to everyone. All set? Blast off, Houston, we have a fun fact: An "independent comprehensive review panel" reported that as of 2010 the cost to develop, launch, and maintain the Hubble Space Telescope, was around ten *billion* dollars.[1] Not unrelated to this is another government report which reveals that around ten *million* people visit Niagara Falls each year.[2] Having a hard time deciding how these two big numbers are related? Simple. Whether we're looking around the cosmos or looking around our backyard, we've got a thing for creation. If we want to see water fall it's as simple as turning on a kitchen faucet. Yet, ten million visitors each year will spend time and money to stand on the shores of the Niagara River and watch water fall in a *big* way. Yep, we love the grandeur of creation. It's in our nature to feel connected to nature.

Given the glories of creation, it's no wonder that we see a connection between the Creator and creation. Long before the

Hubble Telescope, the author of Psalm 19 declared: "The heavens are telling the glory of God; and the firmament proclaims his handiwork."[3] This psalm asserts that nature exposes God's fingerprints; that creation is the revelation of God's "handiwork." Here we encounter an area of theology that explores how God is revealed in the natural order. This is an important approach for those who want to link theology and the natural sciences. For proponents, our experience of nature becomes a common language used to highlight attributes of God's character, or even to defend God's very existence. Thomas Aquinas (ca. 1225-1274) wrote that "from the effects of his creation we know of God that he is, and that he is the cause of other beings, super-eminent above other beings, and removed from all."[4] Thomas had a way with words; he certainly used enough of them. That's not a bad thing considering how many of us are left speechless by the beauty of creation.

The apostle Paul went so far as to say that creation is such a blatant tip-off that God exists, that ignorance of God's existence is essentially an inadmissible plea. In his letter to the church in Rome, Paul states that nature has openly informed the guilty and the wicked of God's divinity:

> What can be known about God is plain to them, because God has shown it to them. Ever since the creation of the world his eternal power and divine nature, invisible though they are, have been understood and seen through the things he has made. So they are without excuse. (Rom. 1:19-20).

Paul isn't allowing any wiggle room: "Open your eyes buckos, our invisible God is visible in nature and you know it!" (okay, I'm loosely paraphrasing). This might be an indicator of why Paul took up a career in preaching and not labour relations. I must say though, that I would want Paul to be my union representative: "Creation obviously tells us that outdoor picnic tables are needed at every processing plant and you know it" (this time I'm loosely fabricating). Paul, like Thomas Aquinas, had a pretty high opinion of nature. Neither of them called created matter a pointer, but they were happy to point out that nature points our attention towards God. Point taken.

It must be stressed that we're focusing on God, not on nature. The connection between the pointer (nature) and the pointee (God) must not be distorted. God and creation are separate and distinct. Augustine of Hippo (354-430) was clear about this in his personal account of seeking out God. He even made an inventory of nature's refusal to be mistaken for God:

> What is it that I love? I asked the earth, and it said, 'It's not me,' and everything in it admitted the same thing. I asked the sea and the great chasms of the deep, and the creeping things that have the breath of life in them, and they answered, 'We aren't your God: search above us.' … I asked the sky, the sun, the moon, the stars, and they said, 'We're not the God you're looking for, either.' … I asked the whole huge universe about my God, and it answered me, 'I am not God, but God made me.'[5]

Augustine is a bit of a chipmunk philosopher here. His wisdom is offered with enough tongue-in-cheek to inflate the cheekiest chipmunk face. Oddly enough, I picture him more as a chip*monk*. He's virtuous and his intentions are spot-on. Augustine knew that some folks had fallen into worshiping nature; elevating nature into a Creator/creation mash-up. This distorted idea, known as pantheism, views God and the universe as being identical. This is about as far away as you can get from the idea that creation points away from itself, and to its Creator. Pantheists just don't get the whole point of pointers. Christians worship a *who*, not a *what*. Once again,

Augustine countered this confusion and set the matter straight:

> God alone is to be worshiped who is the creator of all things that are, from Whom, by Whom, unto Whom are all things, that is, the unchanging Source, unchanging Wisdom, unchanging Love, One True and Perfect God, who never was not, never will not be; never was other, never will be other; than whom nothing is more hidden, nothing more present; with difficulty we find where he is, with greater difficulty, where he is not; with whom all cannot be, without whom no one can be.[6]

As the fiery pastors say: *Can I get an amen!* This is pure proclamation. Augustine puts first things first. The crux of the matter is that it's alright to hug a tree; they bark but they don't bite. Just remember that you're hugging a gift – not the Giver of the gift. Noticing gifts is at the heart of orienting ourselves to the Giver. In this way, noticing has a lot in common with worshiping. It is engagement – noticing isn't passive. When we notice material pointers in reference to God, we are actively defining the essence of our humanity. Our humanity emerges in tandem with our orientation to God. That makes noticing a big ongoing part of being human before God.

When we talk about creation and tree-gifts, we're usually talking about material stuff – what our scientist friends call "matter." Take a moment to conjure up mental images of material pointers. - - -*think, think, conjure, conjure, think*- - - What comes to mind? There's plenty to choose from. Matter could be marbles, or rocks, or pancakes, or piccolos, or particles. Sure, it could be a lot of stuff – *all* stuff, actually. It can even be human stuff, like … well, humans. Technically, people are created matter. Of course, we are so much more, but our matter matters. We (you and me and everyone), are unique pointers. When other people encounter *us*, everything about us is encountered in reference to God. Because "us" really means every single person; this is a universal phenomenon. Everyone else sees you in reference to God *and* you see everyone else in reference to God. Think of God as the background of every image that enters your field of vision. Have I freaked you out yet?

Karl Rahner provided an excellent framework to explore this fundamental idea. He was a particularly thinky German fellow, so he used a thinky German phrase for the overall concept: *Vorgriff auf esse* (or commonly, just *Vorgriff*). In English, this is usually translated with a single word: pre-apprehension. Let's break this single word down. Apprehension is the grasping or seizing of an object or a concept. It's a versatile word that is also used to communicate reaching out to seize - to apprehend – a criminal. We're not criminals, so we're only concerned with the combined physical and mental steps we use to acquire and understand: We apprehend so that we might comprehend. If we want to spell out how we arrive at comprehension, we can say that apprehension precedes comprehension, and *pre*-apprehension occurs prior to apprehension. Think of pre-apprehension as an instant that initiates the orientation of our *being* towards the object we are reaching for – the object we are engaging to apprehend. We do this as part of our very existence. It's part of our *being* human beings. Because we are human beings and matter that, like all pointers, refer to God, our very being reaches out to God. God is uniquely the Creator of our being. We have human being, but God *is* absolute being. God's being is the fullness of possible being.

Rahner's work suggests that when apprehending an object, our relation is never solely with that particular object. We are, at the same time, reaching beyond the particular towards "absolute being," which is God. Every apprehension is an encounter by which humankind seeks, or *reaches beyond*, to encounter God. That's it in a nutshell. It's this ongoing reaching toward God in the apprehension of objects and concepts that we're calling *pre-apprehension*. This constant referential relationship to God isn't something we are born with. It's not part of our human nature. It's a gift from God that helps us notice the constant presence of God, and it is always there beyond everything that points to God. This is a picture of God, not just *in* the background, but *as* the background.

Hopefully the connection between pointers and Rahner's concept of pre-apprehension is rising to the surface. It is really important to our entire noticing journey. If you're like me and tend to misplace your keys or your morning smile (until the morning coffee works its magic), there is another feature worth noting. Pre-apprehension is the ultimate in portable theories. Our orientation to God is always with us; it simply can't be misplaced. You'll never have to go to the dry cleaners to check whether you've left your pre-apprehension in your jacket pocket. We can't shake pre-apprehension, which is why thinking about it always reminds me of the horizon. In their own ways, pre-apprehension and the horizon share similar attributes. They're always at hand yet always oriented beyond. Thinking about our relationship to the horizon is a helpful way to engage and appreciate the idea of God as the background beyond every encounter.

We have a reassuringly constant and stable relationship with the horizon. When we move towards the horizon, we are aware that there is a distance we cannot bridge. No need to get in a huff about it; we've come to accept it. If we start driving towards the horizon at breakfast, no one in the back seat asks "Are we there yet?" come lunchtime, or ever. Like this, the idea of *arriving* at God is silly. In our lifetime we are always journeying toward God. Be wary of those who claim to have caught up with God (at least until they demonstrate how to arrive at the horizon).

Thinking about pre-apprehension
reminds me of the horizon

Each of us lives with the horizon on a daily basis. It is always there, so we can fairly easily imagine it even when it is hidden from us. Walking in the center of a city crowded with skyscrapers, we probably can't see the horizon line. Yet, we know it is there beyond the buildings that corral us. That's just like pre-apprehension reaching out towards God. Even when life gets cluttered up with skyscraper-sized busyness or worry, our encounters with God are ongoing. They are constantly there whether we see them or not, or perceive God to be distant, or near. Similarly, just because the horizon is always beyond, doesn't mean it always appears to be at the same distance. From experience we can picture it being close, and we can picture it as distant. Standing on the coast overlooking open ocean the horizon is way off in the distance. Standing in a field at the foot of a hill, the horizon appears almost within reach. Either way, the horizon is always a *beyond* reference point. Every moment of life is lived on this side of the horizon. In this sense we live within the horizon. Every thing, thought, experience and action in life shares this common reality:

All have a relationship to the horizon. All are reference points to the horizon.

Look at the last two sentences one more time. If we drop in "God" each time it reads "the horizon," the connection between pointers and pre-apprehension comes into focus. When we see pointers, like my garbage bin, we pre-apprehend that it exists in relation to God. And like the horizon that meets the sky, this activity is an ongoing facet of our everyday existence that we seldom consciously notice.

Looking at it from a different angle, there is no shortage of things we *do* notice. We definitely notice the stuff we like to put our hands on. It is fair to say that material pointers get most of the limelight because we've got a thing for materiality. When we put our hands on stuff, for example a piano, a lot more is going on than just the sensation of touching the (hopefully imitation) ivory keys. There are cognitive things going on. Basically, we can't stop ourselves from thinking. Encountering any thing or idea means engaging with it at some level. I may touch the piano keys, but I'm also analyzing the sensation of contact, appraising the sound produced, and forming opinions. In doing so, I'm accepting and rejecting a variety of potential responses and, very likely, recognizing my personal reaction. If I have a predetermined idea of what I creatively and emotionally desire from the piano, that will shape my experience and my response. In fact, it seems downright impossible to completely separate my physical and cognitive engagement with the piano. No wonder then, that the same holds true for pointers. That's why the sight of my garbage bin, my recognition of the design function, and my sensory reaction to the smell were intertwined.

Although material and cognitive encounters coincide, we can appreciate the unique aspects of cognitive pointers. For instance: I am blessed to have four wonderful sisters-in-law. It is a good thing there are four. There's safety in numbers and I *really* don't want to single anyone out here – I'm not naming names. The fact is that one of my sisters-in-law makes a pronounced snorting noise when she laughs. I'm not referring to a run of the mill garden variety snort. No, when she laughs, she is possessed by a joyous sputtering squeal that turns heads and bewitches livestock – to put it gently. Laughing is one of the supreme examples of material and cognitive pointers co-existing. The cognitive faculties spasm out and the material body (nose in this case) can't resist aurally guffawing. I maintain that, though my dear sister-in-law makes a snooticious racket, it is the joy of the laughter that overtakes her. Her cognitive delight far outpaces her aural celebration. There is no mistaking the singularity of the cognitive pleasure that accompanies each snort-pointer. It is a clear reminder that the author of our lives is ultimately the author of our laughter. There is something theologically significant in laughter. Rahner reckons that "Laughter is praise of God because it foretells the eternal praise of God at the end of time, when those who must weep here on earth shall laugh"[7] (check out Luke 6:21 for more blessed details).

Some aspects of cognitive pointers are as obvious as a ski hill in Saskatchewan; they stand out. Others are of a more subtle ilk. Both the obvious and the obscure warrant our notice, because *everything points to God*. To illustrate this, let's shift our attention to two stalwarts of poetry: Shakespeare, and the poets at a well-known Swedish furniture store. The Bard of Avon is up first with the first four lines of his Sonnet 98:

> From you have I been absent in the spring,
> When proud-pied April dress'd in all his trim
> Hath put a spirit of youth in every thing,
> That heavy Saturn laugh'd and leap'd with him.

Hmm ... nice. Next up is an excerpt from a Scandinavian furniture assembly manual:[8]

Perhaps this side-by-side comparison isn't entirely fair. Shakespeare tried his best but really can't compete with the Swedish Masters for pure cognitive engagement. Not convinced? Think of the last time you engaged with a furniture assembly manual. Sure, the two-step desk lamp instructions are simple enough, but how about the ultra tricky GRUNTLÄTELI electric dresser with faucet? Okay, I made that up. It seems best not to enrage Swedish readers by singling out a specific "ready-to-assemble" flat-pack nightmare. The point is that anyone who has had to second (or third) guess the meaning of 27-step smiling man furniture assembly hieroglyphics gets this. Navigating the steps involves heightened cognitive engagement guided only by nonverbal hints. In their poetic subtlety and our interactive angst, the well-meaning minds who design the manuals *and* the minds that decipher them, actively point to God. Shakespeare's bit isn't too bad either. All three endeavours evidence gifts that are essential facets of our spiritual lives.

Rahner didn't write about Swedish furniture, but he certainly celebrated the ingenuity behind their assembly manuals. His *Prayer for Creative Thinkers* addresses "O Father of Poets" and the "Spirit of all True Inspiration." He petitions God to "Raise up among us men endowed with creative powers, thinkers, poets, artists. We have need of them!"[9] Noticing the connection between our cognitive gifts and the origin of all gifts, reminds us afresh of the connection between intellect and spirit. Commenting on the significance of this link, Rahner cautioned that "there can in the long run be no really spiritual life without an intellectual life."[10] Let's cast around to see if anyone else seconds this motion.

Looking back for a few nips of monastic wisdom, it's fair to say that Bonaventure (1221-1274)[11] and Francis of Assisi (ca. 1181-1226) noticed cognitive and material pointers. Curiously, they didn't call their references to God pointers (I'll cut them some slack on this oversight). That aside, both men exhibited keen appreciation for the signposts of God in their lives. Bonaventure was a Franciscan theologian and philosopher with a pronounced mystical inquisitiveness. In his milestone work, *The Journey of the Mind to God* (or *Itinerarium Mentis in Deum* for you picky Latin readers), Bonaventure reflects on cognitive functions as a means to know God exists. This is possible, he suggests, because an "image" of God is accessible through reflection on the infinite being of God (I did hint that he was all about the mystical). This is a bit like Rahner's proposal that limited human *being* reaches out for the perfection of unlimited God.

One of the keys for us is Bonaventure's frequent use of a mirror metaphor. He uses it in *The Journey of the Mind to God* to help readers envision the universe as a mirror in which traces of God can be seen. With this he outlines the steps to be taken to encounter God. Of course, my short description greatly reduces the grandeur of his mystic mysticalness. Let's go to the source and let Bonaventure comment on encountering God through the traces of creation and our five senses. Here's a snippet:

> [By following the steps] we are led to seeing God in his traces, as if we had two wings falling to our feet, we can determine that all creatures of this sensible world lead the mind of the one contemplating and attaining wisdom to the eternal God; for they are shadows, echoes, and pictures, the traces, simulacra, and reflections of that First Principle most powerful, wisest, and best; of that light and plenitude; of that art productive, exemplifying, and ordering, given to us for looking upon God.[12]

The Cognitive and Experiential bottom line: Bonaventure's mind and senses noticed the constant offer of God.

Francis of Assisi was the much beloved founder of the Order of Friars Minor, now commonly known as Franciscans. His connection to the gifts of creation is the stuff of legend. This is witnessed in the imagery of Francis' famous *Canticle of Brother Sun and Sister Moon*. He was, quite seriously, known to preach to animals, who he invited along with all creation to praise God. There are many wonderful stories about Francis of Assisi's connection to animals. Perhaps the best known is the tale of Francis taming a ferocious wolf that had been terrifying the citizens and livestock of Gubbio, in Italy. The underlying feature of these stories is Francis' understanding that animals, and all of creation, exist in relation to God. Francis' thirteenth-century biographer, Julian of Speyer, recorded that "The mind of blessed Francis was filled with such great sweetness of divine love that, because he saw the marvelous work of the Creator in all things, he abounded in the greatest tenderness of piety towards all creatures."[13]

The Material bottom line: Francis saw the world around him and noticed the constant offer of God.

Before going forward, we're going to go back a wee bit further. Before Bonaventure and before Francis, Augustine shared his own enduring insights into the deeply personal impact noticing can have on a person. At the close of the fourth-century Augustine wrote: "You struck my heart to the core with your Word and I fell in love with you. But the sky, too, and the earth, and everything that's in them – look, from all directions everything is telling me to love you, and never stops telling all people."[14]

When we departed on this journey it seemed reasonable that, at least initially, some readers would look askance at the idea that everything points to God. It's quite possible that some folks even shook their heads and flipped to the back cover to check out my academic credentials. Rest assured, I'm totally fine with that. In our fake news era, we all have to make sure we're not being taken for a ride to some weird gated theological compound at the edge of town. Sometimes suspicion buddies up to common sense and asks, "Are you buying this?" Such a response makes total sense to me. I wouldn't have pitched *everything* as a "big bang" idea if I didn't think it would explode a few brain cells. Big bangs do just that. One of the reasons that the apostle Paul, Augustine of Hippo, Bonaventure, Francis of Assisi, Thomas Aquinas and Karl Rahner have turned up in these pages, is to help make sense of the legitimacy of noticing pointers. Noticing and pointers are not just catch words used to push a gimmick book. By ditching chronological snobbery, we have opened our journey up to input from a diverse group of acknowledged church leaders from across multiple eras. This is how the church keeps on track. It is how we make sure our theological ideas have substance. Inviting the input of established historical voices is particularly important when we have sweeping ideas like *everything* points to God.

I have discussed pointers in one guise or another with many people. When folks think about everything pointing to God long enough, it seems that just about everyone eventually arrives at the same bigtime serious challenge: What about evil? If everything points to God, then evil points to God! How can this possibly make sense?

Evil isn't an elusive idea. Sadly, there is ample evidence of it. On any given day there are heart-breaking reports of hate crimes, oppression, exploitation, and violence perpetrated by humans, against humans. At our best we challenge and oppose evil, yet we never truly banish it. As Rahner describes it, "this world is a divided world. It is not merely a creation of God that has perhaps failed to achieve its fully earthly perfection. This world in which culture, humanity, and the creative design of

God are to be realized is also a world in which there is evil and darkness and hell."[15] Rahner's theology is, on the whole, very optimistic. At its core, his work displays a distinctly positive view of the capacities God has gifted us. Yet, his theology also makes it clear that real optimism is not escapism. If all that is good references God, then we need to wrestle with how all that is wicked references God. If celebration references God, how does suffering do the same?

Wrapping our heads around this involves considering how central comparisons are to our everyday thought processes. Here's a common example: I'm standing at the sink in my kitchen washing dishes. As you walk into the room, I throw you a towel and say, "Give me a hand here." From experience, you know that you will need a dry towel when I hand you dishes from the sink. When you catch the towel, how will you know if it is dry? - - - - No, this isn't a trick question. You can know the dish towel is dry only by knowing it is *not* wet. To understand if something is dry, we must reference our understanding of wet. We unconsciously do comparisons like this all the time. With the towel we referenced an opposite concept, but sometimes more subtlety is required. Not all comparisons are black and white; sometimes they are black and red. Still, the same process of apprehension is in play. We can differentiate the characteristics of red from black even if we need to reference the whole rainbow to do it. It is just a more elaborate way of grasping what something is, by referencing what it is not. Another way to describe this is to say we determine what is present by referencing what is not present. I know wet is present because dry is not present. Could it be that evil is present because good is not present? If so, I cannot identify evil without referencing good. God is the source of good, and indeed, the very definition of good. We know degrees of goodness or evil in relation to absolute good. God is absolute goodness. All good *and* all evil are understood in reference to God. In notice-speak, they point to God.

This observation is not an innovation dreamed up on an exotic noticing expedition. The fundamental idea goes back at least as far as the third-century. A prominent example can be found in the writings of Augustine. He was keenly aware that the biblical claim that God created everything from nothing raises a difficult question. If there was nothing, why is there now evil? Did God create evil? Augustine came to the conclusion that evil is not a created thing. Rather, evil is the name we have given to the absence of good.[16] He reasoned that if evil is a deprivation of good then it cannot be a created thing. Again, this is a way of defining something in reference to what it is not. In this case, evil is defined by the good that is missing. We can't imagine evil without referencing good. Good is defined by God. Pointers all 'round!

If it feels like we're going in circles, take heed, we are not. When it comes to noticing, there is one thing we can be certain of: constancy. Because all things point to God, we run into that fact continually. We're not going in circles and repeatedly coming *back* to the point where we can see pointers; we've never left them. Once we are aware of them, they simply cannot go away. This can lead to real noticing fatigue. Living with an understanding that everything encountered in everyday life exists in relation to God is, at times, overwhelming. Should it be anything less? Of course not. It does mean, however, that consciously noticing requires coping skills. For me, coping means finding the balance between consciously noticing, and unconsciously appreciating. I notice the references to God I encounter to a variety of depths. Some get serious attention, some get an acknowledging nod, and others just form an everyday field of references that I walk among. Each breath is an encounter, but most of us would go crazy if we focused on each breath as a reference to God. Balance is key, and it's not hard to mix things up and maintain a healthy balance.

Question time: Are you with me?

For those who are curious but not yet convinced, the constant offer of God offers us constant opportunity. Rahner had this to say about the potential of noticing:

> If we saw things as they are and experienced human life as it is in reality, then these things, the whole of life, would tell us, as it were, that it is all from God. Then we would perceive the incompleteness of all that is not God, catch the deeper meaning behind things, without which they remain tentative and even pointless – much ado about nothing. Only God in things gives them their fullness, their significance, their orientation.[17]

For those who are, to varying degrees, already appreciating that all of life is lived in relation to God, the next question is obvious. Why?

3

Revelation
(and the Art of Mediation)

There was a time in the not too distant past, when the local schoolyard was the number one source of misinformation for kids. At least it seemed that way in the *My Three Sons* era I grew up in. *My Three Sons* was an oh-so-wholesome television show that ran an astounding twelve seasons (1960-1972). The latter end of the run coincides with my earliest primary school years. I was just old enough to be a fourth son, but was never invited to audition. The situation of this "situation comedy" revolved around the home of a widower, his three sons (obviously not including me), and a live-in housekeeper. Fred McMurray portrayed the wholesome TV dad. Like all decent TV dads, McMurray would occasionally need to have a heart-to-heart conversation with one of his sons. You know the schtick: McMurray would pass on fatherly wisdom about the opposite sex or dealing with bullies. Righteous homespun truths were dished out, just as before on *Ozzie & Harriet* and later on *Happy Days*. Such talks were needed, so that good kids didn't have to "pick it up in the schoolyard." Apparently, the misinformation kids shared over softball games at lunch could subvert all that is good and true in the land of the free. In 1972 Paul Simon elevated this threat to an artform, when he sang his ode to "me and Julio down by the schoolyard." Julio was a posterchild for lawless, unsupervised, and misinformed youth. Strange as it may now seem, the TV and radio of my youth told me that the schoolyard was a lair of bad information and dastardly deeds.

Thanks to the internet, we no longer hear much complaining about the schoolyard. Today kids can access plenty of misinformation without the bother of leaving home. It's the ultimate in misinformation convenience! That doesn't mean that the internet is inherently bad, any more than the schoolyard of my youth was inherently bad. Most people understand the distinction between the schoolyard environment, and the kids who whisper naïve untruths within it. Similarly, we see that the internet is an environment of interconnected computer networks, and that its misinformation originates with individual authors and posters. We no longer need a heart-to-heart with Fred McMurray to distinguish a portal from a posting. Applying this lesson to our notice-quest, we can see that pointers behave a lot like internet portals. Pointers are not information; they convey information. They are like messenger-representatives that point beyond themselves to God. Of course, every rule has its exception – we'll run into one shortly.

To really wrap our heads around the *why* behind pointers, we need to take a closer look at the connection between mediation and revelation. Revelation is God's self-disclosure to humankind. Some theologians find it helpful to use categories to illustrate the scope of God's self-disclosure. The two primary categories used are known as general revelation and special revelation. True, all revelation of God is special, but in this instance "general" doesn't mean *not special*. These grouping names make sense if we consider who each category of disclosure is revealed to. General revelation (sometimes called *natural revelation*), refers to the facets of God's self-disclosure that are available to all people at all times. This grouping includes whatever is revealed about God through the physical universe, through history, and through the makeup of human nature. This list leaves out the self-disclosure of God that is particular to unique times, places and events. These are associated with special revelation; self-disclosure that is not *directly* available to everyone at all times. Some instances of special revelation, like God's self-disclosure to Abraham or Moses, are revealed in scripture. Their written accounts reiterate, and therefore reveal, aspects of God's particular revelation. Yet such accounts are not, strictly speaking, universal disclosures like general revelation, nor are they the particular experiences lived by Abraham and Moses. Trying to categorize revelation is a tricky business. The more we think about God's self-disclosure, the more we grasp how difficult it is to even envision the scope and variety of God's revelation. At the end of the day, when our aching brains need to rest, there is one thing we can be certain of: revelation is communication. God's self-disclosure to us communicates God's *self* – God as God is. Simply put, God is never other than God, so God's self-disclosure never reveals other than God.

Taking time to define just what revelation is and isn't helps us refine what pointers are and aren't. Pointers are universally available to all people, but they are not general revelation. They refer to God, so that we may engage God's self-disclosure. Pointers may be particular to an individual person, but they are not special revelation. Even if a person has an original thought (an oh-so ultra-rare occurrence), it remains a reference to God, so that we may engage God's self-disclosure. If we got together to play a game of Jeopardy, all of the answers (in the form of a question, please) would be "who is God." All of the questions asked would be pointers. That's because pointers are signposts that direct our attention to God's revelation – they pose the questions that are satisfied in God's revelation. *I'll take pointers for five-hundred, Alex!*

The link between pointers and revelation is coming into focus. Pointers do not reveal, they reference God, who is continually revealing and revealed. What remains to be sorted is the link between pointers and mediation. Let's use a cringeworthy story to help define the essence of mediation. Suppose you are a ridiculously big fan of *NSYNC. I'm not accusing anyone of boyband tendencies here; this is strictly to make a point. Anyway, you are on a mission to stage a massive *NSYNC reunion concert. When you make your pitch to each member of the group, your biggest obstacle becomes obvious. It's Justin, right? All of the other guys (whose names the rest of us may have forgotten), are excited about the reunion. Justin Timberlake, however, is a hold-out.[1] He has outgrown that awkward boyband tag and actually has a thriving adult career. There are now two camps to bring together: Justin, and the other nameless guys. To stage the big reunion show you've got to bring these two camps together – mediation is needed. Mediation is the process of bringing two separate entities together.

Shifting from *NSYNC-quest to our notice-quest, the question at hand is: Do pointers bring separate entities together? Can we say that pointers mediate between people and God? The answer is a straightforward *Yes-Maybe-No*. No, because the material and cognitive pointers we've focused on do not mediate God's revelatory presence. Maybe, because there are Christian liturgical traditions that acknowledge God's presence mediated through – or in the company of – material objects. Yes, because (think back to chapter two) people are matter, and as such, material pointers. Most fortunately for us, there is one person who handles the mediation of God and humanity for all humankind. This person is, of course, Jesus of Nazareth.

We all know that any student who answers a direct question with a schizophrenic Yes-Maybe-No response, isn't going to be invited to join the varsity debate team. In fact, my teachers from kindergarten on up would all call me to account:

"Explain yourself, young man." Fair enough, that's exactly what I'm going to do. For starters, the No answer needs no unpacking. No means no means no means no. The Maybe response will take us on an Eastern excursion, so we'll set it aside and tackle Yes first.

Jesus of Nazareth is uniquely the only person in history to be both a meditator between humankind and God, *and* the unmediated presence of God on earth. To say that Jesus points to God may sound more than a wee bit shallow to some readers. There is a tendency in many church communities to hold the divinity of Jesus so high above his humanity, that any stress on Jesus-the-human-person begins to sound awkward. This is problematic. Acknowledging the true humanity of Jesus is not the same thing as advocating a diminished view of Jesus' divinity. It is absolutely central to Christianity that we embrace both the full divinity and full humanity of Jesus.

In scripture, the author of the Epistle to the Hebrews holds the divinity and humanity of Jesus up side-by-side. In the opening chapter of Hebrews, Jesus' divine authority is front and center. He is identified as "the reflection of God's glory and the exact imprint of God's very being" (Hebrews 1:3). This is immediately followed by a second chapter that highlights the humanity of Jesus. There is no fussing about here with obscure language. Jesus is described as being "flesh and blood," and "like his brothers and sisters in every respect" (Hebrews 2:14-17). Having established this, the author of Hebrews emphasises the role of Jesus as mediator again, and again, and again (Hebrews 8:6. 9:15, 12:24). If the author was around today, he would have a *Jesus is Mediator* blog, podcast, twitter feed, and would definitely be handing out organic cotton *JC Mediates!* T-shirts. That said, I wouldn't go looking for him on *Tik Tok*; he didn't go in for backsliding or falling away dance moves.

All silly-sides aside, the union of divinity and humanity in

Jesus Christ is the essential belief that makes the claims of Christianity coherent. It is the fullness of humanity in Jesus that allows his mediation for all humankind to be our reality. Jesus is the fullest revelation of God, *and* the fullest human acceptance of God's offer of salvation *for* humankind.

When we talk about Jesus being the fullest revelation of God, we are, in other terms, speaking of the fullest self-disclosure of God in human history. What humankind has received with Jesus is the fullest event of *God giving God*. The apostle Paul heralds this when he describes Jesus as "the image of the invisible God" in his letter to the church in Colossi (Colossians 1:15). This isn't loose talk. This is Jesus presented as the *real presence* of God – the invisible made visible. The presence of Jesus is simultaneously the presence of God's mediator, the presence of God disclosing God, and God's self-offer to creation. Let's face it, this is God's world, so God communicates exactly what God desires to communicate. And what God has chosen to communicate is … God.

Our Yes-Maybe-No exploration of pointer mediation has taken on some additional gravity. Flying under the radar in all of this, is how Jesus enriches our comprehension of everyday garden-variety pointers. Jesus, as we've noted, addresses us as the offer of God in its fullest revelation. Consequently, because Jesus is the fullest form of God's offer of self, he also reveals the intent of all revelation. *All revelation communicates God's self-offer to us!* The loving breadth of the offer we notice in the life and death of Jesus, is exactly the same offer we engage when pointers prompt us to notice the constant offer of God. Just so the title of this book isn't lost on anyone, what I'm saying is:

THE CONSTANT OFFER IS GOD'S OFFER OF GOD'S SELF TO HUMANKIND.

Like all offers, God's offer is a proposal. Not exactly the matrimonial kind of proposal you see on a baseball scoreboard during the seventh inning stretch … but there are similarities.[2] Both types are proposals that, once communicated, hang in the air. Offers like this propose an everlasting union; they command attention and can't be ignored indefinitely. They are joyfully serious, and like all questions, are not resolved until an answer is given. Once you have received a proposal, the ball is in your court. A scoreboard proposal is ultimately a self-offer. When someone has laid themselves bare by proposing, you, as the recipient, are given an awesome life-changing power: the power to accept or reject. Hope abounds that the proposals we see in baseball stadiums end with a heartfelt embrace. Ditto for God's proposal … the one that hangs on the edge of every pointer … constantly.

The connection between revelation and mediation has huge importance for us. Jesus, it turns out, is pivotal to our exploration of pointers. His presence is a game-changer. With Jesus in the pointing equation, we can no longer think of pointers merely as sign-posts that direct our attention to God. Now we must tackle the question of pointers as divine presence. If Jesus is both the ultimate pointer and the real presence of God among us, can lesser pointers also be aligned with real presence? Because the massive connotations of this question are too big to take on in one bite, I vote that we aid our cerebral digestion by narrowing the field a bit. Let's set aside our thoughts about Jesus' continued presence in history, and the questions that raises about the nature of time. That topic can stretch our brains in a later chapter. For now, our journey will focus on the garden-variety material and cognitive pointers we set sail with in chapter two. Friends, we're headed into *Maybe* territory.

Occasionally the big bookstore in my town brings in a children's storyteller on a Saturday afternoon. You have probably seen this kind of thing. There's generally a dramatic storyteller who wants to draw young listeners into their story world. To effectively set the scene at the beginning of their story, the storyteller says something like "Picture this." This does the trick, because the words following the "picture this" invitation take on a new visual scope and depth in each listener's imagination. That's because words strung together as language function like symbols. If I use the word "castle" in a story, it represents something; it isn't merely a written arrangement of scribbles or an aural experience of sound. Simply reading "castle" launches an image of turrets in your mind. Like it or not, there is probably a castle turret floating around in your mind right now. Words make things that are not words present in our consciousness. Symbols, like a good storyteller, can trigger powerful visual images. Photographs epitomize this symbolic power – particularly photos of important people in our lives. Viewing a photographic print of a departed loved one makes a potent glimpse of the essence of that person present. The image communicates things that transcend the material make-up of the paper and chemicals it is comprised of.

For those who are aurally oriented, we can also grasp the idea of presence in musical experience. Most of us can pinpoint a particular song that we associate with a past event or bygone place. Hearing old songs can transport us. It is common to nostalgically say a song takes us back in time, but think about it, aren't things from the past really brought to the present moment? This makes a song a symbol, much in the same way a photograph is. Photographs and songs make a good case for the capacity of material and cognitive pointers to function like symbols. This is a more intricate way of envisioning pointers. So far, we have treated material and cognitive pointers like signs that point away from themselves. However, it appears that the symbolic element of pointers can *retrieve* as well as

Symbols make things present
in our consciousness

articulate what a sign can only point to. Symbols have a point.
There are good grounds for this claim. The philosopher Louis
Dupré has written extensively about symbols and signs. In his
view, symbols articulate the signified, meaning that they have
an independence from the signified. This allows symbols to
have a mediating capacity that signs do not have. This is,
Dupré says, a characteristic that differentiates signs and symbols.[3] Signs, which I've more specifically called "signposts,"
may point to the signified or may represent it. Symbols can
mediate.

A few pages back, when the idea of mediation was introduced, the fictional mediator desperately seeking an *NSYNC
reunion was facing an unenviable task. Justin Timberlake was
operating as a separate entity from the remaining unified
(though unnamed) *NSYNCians. This mediator may know
that their task involves bringing together two separate camps,
but do they know they need to follow the example of a symbol,
and not a labour mediator? My guess is, this is news to them
(what with being fictional and all). We all know what happens
if a mediator is brought in to bridge the divide between the
striking members of Cheese Straightener's Local 253 and their
employer, Geometric Cheese Inc. Once the mediator has
helped negotiate a coming-together of the two camps, they
continue to operate as two entities. Sure, they have an
agreement of sorts, but each camp maintains their own
identity. That won't work for *NSYNC, because they need to
truly be joined at the hip into a singular entity. They must unify
into that in-step posing, singing, and dancing entity that we so
respectfully call a "boyband." SYNCing up a handful of *cute n'*
cheeky lads takes the kind of mediation that is inherent in
symbols. Dupré explains it this way:

> An exclusively concept-oriented way of thinking has
> accustomed us to conceive of a symbol as extrinsically
> connecting two things which are essentially different, in

the manner of an allegory or a simile. But a true symbol intrinsically unifies the elements of which it is constituted.[4]

In short, Dupré is saying that a true symbol really has the presence of the thing (or person) it points to and represents. If the separate *NSYNC camps consist of the symbol and the signified, this is good news for their fans. More significantly, this reveals an important potential in noticing-pointers. I'm talking about mundane pointers that represent divine presence. Different Christian traditions have reached different conclusions about this possibility. We've finally arrived at the heart of the Maybe response.

The veneration of icons is an intrinsic part of the liturgical life of the Eastern Orthodox Church.[5] Icons are brilliantly coloured artistic images that convey divine presence.[6] Some portray Jesus, or scenes recorded in scripture. Other icons portray saints of the church. We're chiefly concerned with artistic representations of the Holy Trinity. For example, a Trinity icon may have an image or symbolic representation of Jesus, alongside symbolic indicators of the presence of God the Father and the Holy Spirit. Icons are highly stylized images, created in prayerful devotion, and without any intention of capturing a likeness of God's unrenderable nature or essence Aside from the acknowledged impossibility of this, the Eastern Orthodox tradition places significant stress on divine mystery.

Many Western Christians have a sketchy understanding of icons. When assessing the place of icons in Christian life, it is important to recognize that icons are not worshiped. Rather, they are revered and treated with the respect properly accorded to their subjects and their liturgical significance. While it is true that many Christian traditions have used images to teach aspects of the faith, icons are substantially different from stained glass or statuary. They don't just tell a story; they are celebrated as symbolic representations that bring earth and heaven together (like earthly windows into heaven). In a similar manner to Dupré's conception of symbols, icons bring symbolic presence and real presence together. Alexander Schmemann (1921-1983) was an Orthodox priest and influential teacher in North America. He described icons as material symbols which allow viewers to participate in the meeting of mundane reality and divine reality:

> [I]t is the very nature of symbol that it reveals and communicates the 'other,' the visibility of the invisible *as* invisible, the knowledge of the unknowable *as* unknowable, the presence of the future *as* future. The symbol is the means of knowledge of that which cannot be known otherwise, for knowledge here depends on participation – the living encounter with and entrance into that 'epiphany' of reality which symbol is.[7]

It is evident from Schmemann's comments that icons belong in our conversation about pointers. Although the designation "pointer" is wholly foreign to the Eastern Orthodox lexicon, the common ground is plain to see. Like pointers, the significance of an icon must be noticed and embraced by the viewer. For some, icons are venerable symbols, and for others they are appreciable only in the realm of art. Recognizing that these divergent views co-exist in Christianity, let's return to our questions: do pointers bring separate entities together, *and* do pointers mediate between people and God? We have covered the definitive Yes response that is grounded in the uniqueness of Jesus. Now, with the introduction of icons, I hope the Maybe response makes a bit more sense. Of course, there are readers who are still wondering why I tossed aside the No option like a vegan responding to a McHappy Meal. After all, isn't Maybe really just a decision parfait made with equal parts Yes and No?

The Church has a longstanding uneasiness with the notion of venerating humanly-crafted images of deity. The display of icons has historically created division in both the Eastern and Western Christian traditions. For some, the acceptance of icons appears to contradict the multitude of prohibitions against idols in scripture. In the Byzantine East, opposition to icons fueled two protracted periods of division.[8] A wave of iconoclasm (a term derived from the Greek words for "smashing of images"), prompted the Byzantine Emperor Leo III the Isaurian to issue an edict forbidding the veneration of images in 730. Those who upheld the display of icons were persecuted. It took over a century for the controversy to be officially settled. At the risk of sounding like a stuffy history professor, I think a few snippets from the debate are worth recalling. The following two excerpts give us insight into the value of icons in the eyes of their proponents.

The Eighty-Second decree of the Trullan Synod (692):

In venerating the ancient icons and the saints who were devoted to the Church, as symbols and as prototypes of the Truth, we especially venerate grace and truth as the fulfillment of the Law. Therefore, that what has been accomplished may be represented to all men's eyes through the art of painting. We decree that henceforth there are to be imprinted upon the icons of Christ our God … his Words, to bring to mind his life in the flesh, his Passion, his saving Death, and the redemption of the whole world which has proceeded therefrom.[9]

The Second Council of Nicaea (787) was the seventh (and final) council that represented both the Western Church centered in Rome, and the Eastern Church centered in Constantinople. This ecumenical council reinstated the right of churches to display icons. It also bequeathed to subsequent generations a marvelous description of icons as word-like images that can communicate – or mediate – the gospel message:

> Just as all men receive salvation from the syllables contained in the gospels, so also all men, learned and ignorant alike, receive their share of the boon through the channel of the coloured images placed under their eyes. For that which language says and preaches by means of syllables, that writing says and preaches by means of colours.[10]

The decision of the Second Council of Nicaea would seem to suggest that our Maybe response was officially upgraded to a Yes. In the Eastern Church this verdict holds to today. This is evidenced by the words of Vladimir Lossky (1903-1958), who is often cited as the most significant Orthodox theologian of the twentieth century. A mere seventy-five years ago, Lossky described icons as "holy images which express things in themselves invisible, and render them really present, visible and active." They have, he asserted, "a material centre in which there reposes an energy, a divine force, which unites itself to human art."[11]

In Lossky's view, icons are "material signs of the presence of the spiritual world."[12] This description attributes real (albeit mystical) mediating significance to human art. Although Lossky specifically addressed painted images, his words raise questions about how we treat *all* works of art, and especially intentionally "religious" art. If *everything* points to God, aren't all artworks inherently signposts? Furthermore, if images can mediate presence, can all artwork? The question of matter mediating God's presence was a hot button issue for the sixteenth-century Protestant Reformers. The treatment of images of God also received a lot of airtime. If we're going to give the No response a fair hearing, we'll need to take a brief look at some key influencers of this period.

The denial of the real presence of Christ in the consecrated Eucharist bread administered in the Roman Catholic Mass is a key differentiator of Protestantism. With this in mind, it is understandable that the notion of anything symbolizing God's presence would run against the grain for the Protestant reformers. For this No camp, the idea of material mediation is a non-starter. Striking that from the debate list, the remaining question is whether material images of God are desirable, or even acceptable? Martin Luther (1483-1546) accepted religious images for their instructive and memorial value. In Luther's own words, "If it is not a sin, but good to have the image of Christ in my heart, why should it be a sin to have it in my eyes?"[13] He drew the line at veneration which, along with the worship of images, he fervently condemned.[14] Yet, Luther was fine with an image memorializing the sacrifice of Jesus in the home. For him it was all about the intention and function of the artwork. Consider Luther the moderate in our Reformation sampling.

Two cities in Switzerland typify the most stringent applications of the No ethos. The city of Geneva abolished religious art in churches in 1535. Going still further in the NO direction, all religious images were banned in 1580. Depictions of biblical events could not even be printed in books.[15] The teaching of John Calvin (1509-1564) greatly influenced Genevan civic policy. Calvin condemned the ideas people found revealed in images representing God, calling them "frivolous and false."[16] Under Calvin's watch no artistic adornments (including music to accompany hymns) were endorsed in Genevan Churches, and many images were removed.[17] Calvin did allow that biblical scenes in the home were of "some use for instruction or admonition."[18] However, the depth of his true feelings were put on record when he wrote: "We are similar to God only in our souls, and no image can represent him. That is why people who try to represent the essence of God are madmen."[19]

Opposition to images of God also significantly impacted religious life in Zurich. Here, the political influence of Huldrych Zwingli (1484-1531), and later the teaching of Johann Heinrich Bullinger (1504-1575), fueled a deep suspicion of all visual arts. Both leaders had a hand in the strict ban of religious images from churches in Zurich, and influenced the removal of images in some Northern German cities. The ban in Zurich was not extended to the display of images in homes for decorative purposes.[20]

Taken together, we can see that Reformation era Geneva and Zurich treated objects of art with suspicion. Their condemnation offers a stark contrast to the Eastern Orthodox view of icons as art that invites human participation in divine presence. The Swiss Reformers were sincerely concerned that the reverence of artworks could displace reverence for God. They allowed the danger they saw in the attention given to images, to run roughshod over the promise inherent in artwork. Their negative response is a big No to the symbolic power of art, and the notion that all matter ultimately points to God. This effectively placed limited decorative or pedagogical boundaries around art. In imposing these limitations, I fear that an important tenet of creation was set aside: Created things *do not* compete with God. I find it particularly odd in light of the common concern Luther, Zwingli, and Bullinger had with the *intention* of art images in the home. Surely the value placed on the intentions of the owner of the art should also extend to the intention of the artist. In the home, *and in the church*, images created to glorify God do not compete with God.

Having surveyed the Yes-Maybe-No landscape, I plant my flag on the Yes side. Do pointers bring separate entities together? Yes, the referential function of pointers means that any encounter with a pointer is an encounter with its reference point (which is always God). Even so, it must be acknowledged that encounter and mediation are different things. So then, do pointers also mediate between people and God? I say Yes-always in the unique case of Jesus, and Yes-possibly in respect to all other pointers. Ahhhhh! Not another qualification … enough with the maybe-possibly fence-sitting already! (That's my imitation of the exasperated readers who like their mystery to be straight-up black and white). Okay, I feel your grey-area pain and will go on record with a straight(er) answer. To do that I'm going to have to tell another *eureka-moment* story. Unlike the trashy tale that began our journey, this one doesn't stink. It's an upscale anecdote fit to wrap up our foray into the world of concrete revealing images.

This story takes place in an art gallery in Ottawa. Just like the big bang garbage bin tale I shared with you, this one is truly true and really happened to yours truly. The National Gallery of Canada opened in 1880. I missed the opening. More accurately, I missed *that* opening. The gallery has moved around Ottawa and reopened in new buildings as their collection has grown. I visited the newest shiny glass and concrete location just after it opened in 1988. The building takes up 46,621 square metres and has 12,400 square metres of exhibition space (it's a Canadian institution, so I'm toasting the flag and quoting metric stats. If you're partial to square feet you'll have to do the math). The collection is comprised of more than 75,000 works of art. What I'm saying is that there is an impressive amount of impressive art. Walking through it I discovered, to my amazement, that my favourite installation was … the ductwork. Preposterous? Yes, but you did read that right. The ductwork completely messed with my idea of art. The ventilation ducts and electrical conduit tubes formed really interesting patterns against the charcoal grey concrete ceiling. In my mind I imagined taking one of the old-school gilded gold frames from the Vermeer exhibit and holding it up against the ducts. Eureka! Ductwork = Art! My eyes moved around the ceiling as I tried this framing experiment again and again. What a wake-up call; anything and everything can be art.

This wasn't a big bang sized idea, but it still made a pretty large noise in my head. When I looked at the ducts, I was doing more than merely looking. I was engaging with their place- ment and textures, and their correlation to the conduit and concrete. I *noticed* the richness of the ductwork, and *noticed* that the placement and mounting was not haphazard. I *noticed* that the whole layout was intentional. I *noticed* the ductwork was conceived to aesthetically and functionally exist in the gallery's visual environment. No fooling, I *noticed* a lot and learned a lot. I gained a new level of ductwork consciousness, and have paid attention to the aesthetical value of ductwork ever since.

So, what. Just what does this have to do with anything (except my mental health)? Plenty. You see, I didn't just notice; I noticed that I noticed (sound familiar?). My eureka moment wasn't about noticing new textures and colours and place- ment. It was really about noticing that ductwork had existed my whole life, had always had texture and colour, and had always escaped my conscious engagement. In that way, ductwork was like a lot of things in my life (and possibly yours too). From my perspective, every pointer encounter – even the ductwork variety – has the capacity to enrich us spiritually as a moment in which we embrace our orientation to God. In each encounter we can *intentionally* notice our connection to God. The constant offer of God is there for all of us. We can unconsciously walk past it like ductwork, or we can con- sciously engage God's offer.

I know that my stories may not be your stories, just as my taste in ductwork may not match yours. We're sharing a journey, but we each also live unique journeys. Even so, we're all alike in at least one respect. At one time or another we're all on lookout duty, scanning our world and our lives for the presence of God. You, and me, and everyone who has ever looked for God, has asked this question: Where is God? If we're going to consciously seek to notice God, the presence of God is, indeed, a BIG question. Let's flip the page and ask it together ....

4

Here, There, Everywhere
(and Ever-Where)

Have you ever thought seriously about the ineptitude of the Starship Enterprise crew? If memory serves, they left on a five-year mission in 1966. So much for *boldly* going. How long can it take to seek out new life and new civilizations? They've changed captains, they've redesigned the ship, and still they search. The crew even wasted an entire movie searching for Spock. Earth to Kirk: Take a hint already. Anyone who hides that well doesn't want to be found. Still, they need to keep seeking out. Seeking out is the *raison d'être* of adventurers. Heck, the entire Indiana Jones series is based on looking for lost stuff (did you check under the sofa cushions?). Okay, I should cut these adventure-folk some empathetic slack. Those who live in glass houses shouldn't throw Klingon figurines. Yes, that is what I'm getting at: Even though I joke about intrepid adventurers, I am one … just like you. Don't look so surprised; of course you're all intrepid adventurers. Why else would you be reading this book, and joining in our noticing journey?

Upon reflection, it's obvious that we're on a spiritual adventure safari: we're looking for God. The darndest fact is, most of us aren't entirely sure where to look. We may even think back to Moses with a wee bit of envy. When God was ready to hand down the Ten Commandments, Moses was basically given coordinates. This isn't an exaggeration. It's on record that the Lord said to Moses, "Come up to me on the mountain, and wait there; and I will give you the tablets of stone" (Exodus 24:12). Wow, that made the whole finding God challenge pretty easy for Moses. Even with our modern GPS devices, we don't have a leg up. Without the longitude and latitude tip Moses received, we're a bit unsure how to proceed. Do we type "mountain" into the google maps search box? Skip it, vague searches won't help. Ask any FedEx agent and they'll tell you, "If you don't have the delivery address, we're not taking your parcel." Pointers may be signposts to God, but unless they're engraved with a postal code, couriers don't want to know. Common wisdom states that when you want to get to someone, you *need* to know where they are.

Our *need* is the most frustrating thing about looking for God. In Matthew's gospel account, Jesus says, "Come to me, all you that are weary and are carrying heavy burdens, and I will give you rest" (Matthew 11:28). Oh boy, do we need rest. Jesus has offered us a straight-up generous invitation. We desperately want to come to that place where God is present. We *need* to be present where God is present. And, thank you God, there are times when we find your presence. Sometimes God feels so very close, but our experience with presence is erratic. Sometimes God feels so distant. Even for the most mature, plugged-in, super-spiritual person you know, some-times the presence of God seems so very far away. Ouch.

The Christian life is lived within the tension of nearness and distance. If God is everywhere, where am I when I can't find God? Nowhere? Augustine nailed this when he addresses God as, "you, who are the highest and the most near, the most remote but the most present … existing everywhere in your wholeness and yet no particular place."[1] Augustine doesn't seem to be exhibiting frustration here. It is more like he's driven by a sense of wonder. That is an admirable response, given how overwhelming the notion of God's omnipresence –

God's everywhere presence – can be. Augustine's wonderment angle may actually be the only sensible response. For
example, take a moment to ponder God's rhetorical presence
queries, as communicated through the Old Testament prophet
Jeremiah:

> Am I a God near by...and not a God far off? Who can
> hide in secret places so that I cannot see them? ... Do I
> not fill heaven and earth? (Jeremiah 23:23-24)

I hope you're in wonderment mode, or the "who can hide" bit
might be misunderstood. Leave out the wonderment and, for
some, this takes on a creepy Big Brother vibe. I don't mean the
scripted false-reality show; I mean the fictional Big Brother
character (and symbol) in George Orwell's 1949 dystopian
novel, *Nineteen Eighty-Four*.[2] *That* Big Brother is the opposite of
the message we're pondering. In Jeremiah, God is actually
reminding those who would corrupt Israel, that Israel's God is
no mere idol or minor local deity. Israel's God is the real-deal
omnipotent Creator who is ever-present. Yes, we do live in the
tension of God's nearness and distance ... but don't let the
distance fool you. God is present.

If we want a sense of the comfort that God's everywhere
presence promises, we need only remember Jesus' promise:

> Truly I tell you, if two of you agree on earth about
> anything you ask, it will be done for you by my Father in
> heaven. For where two or three are gathered in my name,
> I am there among them. (Matthew 18:18-20).

This isn't just comforting; this is wonderment fuel. When we
are seeking God, what we perceive as distance is not abandonment. Just as the Apostle Paul told some of the locals in the
Athens town square, "God is not far from each one of us" (Acts
17:28). This is important; really important. Still, knowing that

God is among us doesn't change that we all live in the tension
of nearness and distance. I'm delighted to spread wonderment
news, but I'm not a naïve wonderment cheerleader. Life is not
all lollipops and rainbows, and I've never even seen a unicorn
(I'm beginning to doubt their existence). For all my talk about
noticing, I am painfully aware that sometimes God is hidden;
present, but hidden. This is such an ancient theological concern
that we still use a fancy Latin term to talk about it: *Deus
absconditus* – the hidden God. Theologians even muse about
the "hiddenness" of God; a word-warp most dictionaries
wouldn't touch with a ten-foot participle.

The kicker is that we would never have a sense of God's
hiddenness if we weren't searching. But searching is what we
do. We come from a long line of intrepid adventurers that goes
way back. How far? Big time far; even the prophet Isaiah
exclaimed to the Lord, "Truly, you are a God who hides
himself" (Isaiah 45:15). When it comes to searching, we're in
good company. We're also in wise company. Thomas Aquinas
wrote a beautiful hymn which expresses that, in hiddenness,
God is present and personal. The first verse states:

> *Adoro te devote, latens deitas,*
> *Quæ sub his figuris vere latitas;*
> *Tibi se cor meum totum subjicit,*
> *Quia te contemplans totum deficit.*

Lovely, huh? At least, I think it is (my Latin is a little rusty).
Not to worry, I know the English translation is stunning. To
this day it is still sung in the Roman Catholic Mass to celebrate
Christ's Eucharistic presence.

> I devoutly adore you, hidden deity,
> Who are truly hidden beneath these appearances.
> My whole heart submits to you,

>   And in contemplating you, it surrenders itself
>   completely.

Thomas' words are as beautiful as his intellect is bright. They are devotional and celebratory, though in the excerpt above, the word-picture is incomplete. In the final balance we must also acknowledge the weight of hiddenness, and our hope to one day see the revelation of what now eludes us. Thomas understood this, and in the concluding verse of his hymn we find this plea:

>   Jesus, whom now I see hidden,
>   I ask you to fulfill what I so desire
>   That the sight of your Face being unveiled
>   I may have the happiness of seeing your glory.

Every true quest has difficulty, weariness, and heartbreak. Captain Kirk had to contend with the loneliness of space, and Indiana Jones had to deal with ophidiophobia (fear of snakes). Fictional adventurers have to carry burdens. If they didn't, we would never find them believable. The rest of us, we're stuck being non-fiction adventurers. We have to deal with everyday living, hemmed in between the borders of nearness and distance. This is where we catch divine glimpses, while awaiting the day that hiddenness dissolves into the fullness of revelation. Until that happens, we must be aware that our moments of joyful nearness will surely coincide with a neighbour's moment of anguished distance. In such times we may notice God in each breath, yet utterly fail in our efforts to point out these riches to our neighbour. In our lives we will undoubtably live both sides of the joy/anguish equation. There is, as Karl Rahner has stated, "a distance of God that permeates the pious and the impious, that perplexes the mind and unspeakably terrifies the heart."[3]

At the risk of disturbing some comforting notions of nearness, wonderment also recognizes the weight of nearness. If hiddenness is shrouded in distant mystery, then nearness can be characterized as perceiving the presence of that same mystery. I guess that's why nearness is the surest way to amplify the awe in *awe*some mystery. Rahner highlighted how divine mystery creates a sort of parity between near and distant. In one of his meditations, he prayed:

> What can I say to you, my God? ... Shall I complain because I cannot understand your forbearance and because your ways, O Lord, which we, not you, must tread are so incomprehensibly, hidden and incalculable? But how can I reproach you with your distance, when I find your nearness equally mysterious ....[4]

Sometimes intrepid adventurers climb mountains only to find that, except for altitude, there is little difference between the peak and the low-lying base camp. This is particularly true for Christians zealously seeking that elusive mountaintop experience. Sometimes we have to search closer to home ... a lot closer to home. This idea flips the whole Sci-Fi concept of boldly going *out* into space on its head. It becomes a different type of Sci-Fi, with a boldly going *in* search path. You know, it's kind of like that movie on *Dialing for Dollars*. Whoa, I'd better backtrack here. Let's pry the lid off another time capsule for the Gen X, Y, Millennium Z echo-types who missed *Dialing for Dollars*. Hang tight, we'll dig deep in the capsule and this will all makes sense.

Dialing for Dollars was what passed for late afternoon entertainment before the coaxial "cable" TV explosion.[5] If you watched the show it was likely because, even in a four-channel universe, it wasn't the worst thing on (that would be hometown amateur bowling). The show, as the name suggests, also *occasionally* gave out cash prizes. If you're excited about "jackpots" in the ten to twenty-dollar range, this show was for you. The show's premise was simple: they would show a movie, and call potential viewers at home to quiz them on some simple detail related to that movie (like its title or the name of the lead actor). If they called your home and you answered their question correctly, you won the cash jackpot. The attraction for me wasn't the lucrative payouts; it was the offbeat movies. They showed older (read: cheap) movies, and rebroadcast select favourites semi-regularly. One of these repeat-offender movies was a 1966 Sci-Fi gem called *Fantastic Voyage.*

Throw your Sci-Fi adventure expectations out the window. This is where *Dialing for Dollars* earns its place among my theological influences. You see, *Fantastic Voyage* flips the usual script. The adventure heroes in *Fantastic Voyage* don't exploit technology by going out into space. Rather, they are part of a submarine crew that get shrunk down to microscopic size. The crew, in their shrunken sub, are injected into a human body. Their mission is the removal of a life-threatening blood clot (really, you can't make this stuff up). Along the way they have to induce a cardiac arrest, and one of the crew is almost killed by antibodies. Surely you adventurers can see how this all relates to pointers? - - - - Okay, let's spell it out. In *Fantastic Voyage* the adventure isn't external. It is not about a distant outward search. The search is near; so near that it is actually internal. This search action doesn't point away like material or cognitive pointers. No, a resolution is only possible through the internal presence of the submarine crew. The mission objective is met by means of the sub's absolute proximity to the human being. Everything hinges on an intimate presence that is introduced in an intentional and intimate manner. And this, oddly enough, can help us think about the intimate presence of God in us.

For the rest of this chapter we'll be leaning heavily on Rahner's work. At the heart of his theology is a focus on the absolute nearness of God to humankind. It highlights how the intimate nearness of God opens us up to seek what we often associate with God's infinite distance. In a way it helps us to do some spiritual origami by folding nearness and distance together, so that we may see that they are intertwined. We may in such origami moments notice, as Rahner has said, "that in reality God is close to you, just where you are, if you are open to this infinity. For then God's remoteness is at the same time his unfathomable presence, pervading all things."[6] If that seems a little far out to you, I invite you to consider how well Rahner's statement lines up with a giant among the Church Fathers. More than fifteen-hundred years prior to Rahner, Augustine wrote: "God, infused into the world, fashions it; being everywhere present … By the power of his majesty God creates what he creates; by his presence he governs what he has created."[7] If God is everywhere, there really isn't any distinction between near presence and distant presence. Whether we consciously notice it or not, God's presence is in absolute proximity to us.

Think back to our survey of pre-apprehension (technically known as *Vorgriff* in Rahner's work), in chapter two. You'll recall how every thing or concept that we reach out to engage ultimately refers us to God. God is the reference that is always in the background of our existence – constant like the horizon. We are oriented to God because our human *being* desires the fullest possible being – or absolute being – which is God. Fair enough, but as we shuffled through chapter two, did you find yourself asking, "Why is this so?" How is it that we are *all* oriented to God to whom everything points? It seems kind of far-fetched to think we all agreed to go along with a God-orientation scheme. Let's face it, get any five humans together and they won't agree on which pizza toppings to order.

Perfectly sane people can wave a menu around for hours and still not resolve a divisive pineapple debate. As for larger groups (like say, everyone), consensus just eludes us. Fifty *years* on we can't even agree on a single favourite Beatle (it's George, by the way).[8] It's a cinch then, if we are all orientated to God, it is God who has made this possible.

In order to make sense of human orientation to God, we must begin by making sense of ourselves. Just what exactly is the essence of a human being? It's not uncommon to get a two-prong answer to this question: A human being consists of a body and a soul. Unfortunately, this description is rife with problems. Any dualism that separates a material body from a non-material soul feeds all kinds of misconceptions. One of the most prevalent is that, because bodies degenerate and fail, they are suspect. The roots of this misconception go back at least as far as the early philosopher Plato (ca. 429–347 BC). Subsequent thinkers stretched aspects of Plato's teaching to the point that matter was seen as either contrary to the ideal of goodness, or altogether deprived of goodness. These conceptions of matter, including the human body, were as far removed from the revered forms in creation as could be. These notions planted the seeds for every group that later proclaimed *Soul* = *Good* and *Body* = *Bad* (or whatever language they chose to describe godforsaken bodily depravity).

The problem with this dualistic approach is fairly obvious: God's good creation is a whole lot of matter. We can't justify denigrating the physical materiality of our bodies, any more than we can the very ground we stand on. If we hold that material creation is God's good gift, then so are our bodies. Therefore, we need to recast our thinking to make sense of the physical and spiritual make-up of humanity. This becomes easier to envision when we abandon the baggage associated with body and soul and replace it with categories that more accurately describe human *being*. Let's not overthink this. If we want terms that help us distinguish between the natural and supernatural components of human being, why not just use *natural* and *supernatural*? These terms are straightforward and technically accurate – they check all the boxes. They will also help us better understand some important things about pre-apprehension.

At a certain point in our youth we grasp that we're created beings. It dawns on us that we're natural entities living within a natural ecosystem. Each of us is flesh and bone matter, with all the limitations that implies. Obviously, we are finite. It is our natural condition to wear out and die. We see evidence of this all around us, and consequently, the sane among us figure out that we differ from God. God, being infinite and eternal, transcends the limitations of our finite nature. Thus, we recognize that God is above nature – God is *supernatural.* Okay, the boundaries are set. God has created the natural order, and anything that is supernatural transcends the created order. Any supernatural component of being human is not a part of human nature – we aren't born or created with it. Any supernatural facet of being human must, therefore, be given to us. Only supernatural God can give humanity the capacity to supernaturally transcend our natural limitations.

Don't let the otherworldly sound of "supernatural" freak you out. At the heart of this is God gifting humankind with an orientation to God. Our spiritual drive to reach out to God is a supernatural capacity. Sometimes Rahner referred to this potency in us as human *spirit.* This was his shorthand way of saying we have a capacity to transcend – to reach out beyond the limitations of our nature. Again, we can't let this terminology bog us down. Human *spirituality* is not something we acquire at a weekend seminar. It is the gift of spirit given each of us, orienting us to seek beyond. Our spirituality is human spirit seeking above our natural limitations; seeking the fulfilment of our being in God. Fulfillment in God is what we are reaching for in every act of apprehension. In other words: every time we engage in pre-apprehending a thing or concept, our human spirit is seeking God's revelation. If this is beginning to sound familiar, it should. Bringing human spirit into the mix adds a dimension that amplifies our pre-apprehension introduction in chapter two. Specifically, it fleshes out this passage:

> The ongoing reaching toward God in the apprehension of objects and concepts is what we're calling *pre-apprehension*. This constant referential relationship to God isn't something we are born with. It's not part of our human nature. It's a gift from God that helps us notice the constant presence of God, and it is always there beyond everything that points to God.[9]

It is by seeking God's self-disclosure that we gather our knowledge of God. We must use the term "knowledge" loosely here, keeping uppermost in mind that engaging divine mystery is unlike any other endeavour to "know." Rahner put it this way: "We have enough spirit in us to know God. But what does this mean except that we know we stand before an unfathomable being whose ways are unsearchable and whose judgments are incomprehensible?"[10] When we ask, "Where is God?" we inevitably have to ask questions about God's presence and revelation. It also appears that our *where* question is tightly aligned to the question of knowing God. I may say, "I know God," but what I really mean has more to do with searching out and engaging God's revelation than the conventional acquisition of facts.

If our seeking out and God's revelation are interconnected, which prompts which? In Augustine's enduring *Confessions*, he mused over this chicken/egg-type paradox. Augustine wondered how a person knows to search for God if they do not know God exists. Of course, Augustine was too eloquent to sink to my chicken/egg analogy; instead, he wrote:

> Grant me, Master, to know and understand whether a person ought first to call on you or to praise you; and which of the following is first, to know you or to call on you? But who invokes you without knowing you? In his ignorance, he might call on the wrong thing.[11]

Augustine's question is one for the ages. This paradox echoes a line of inquiry exhibited in one of Plato's dialogues, and it's a definite brain tickler.[12] How can we search for what we do not already know? And if we do search for what we don't know, how will we recognize it should we come across it? We can sort through this muddle if we embrace the assertion that our orientation to God is gifted to us. Working from this basis, Rahner proposed a framework for understanding our orientation to God that unlocks the riddle of Augustine's paradox.

Up to this point we haven't delved too deeply into the *being* aspect of human being. Our *being* is synonymous with the day-to-day reality of our human existence. Rahner suggested that, for humankind, existence is informed by a concept he called the *supernatural existential.* Let's not forget that I introduced Rahner as a "thinky German fellow." That was my shorthand way of saying that, in addition to being a brilliant theologian, he was a formidable philosopher. For readers who care about such things, note that Rahner was influenced by Martin Heidegger. He knew all about the tools lying around the workshops of phenomenology and existentialism. For those of you who aren't keen on Continental philosophy – don't sweat it, you'll still get the point.

Oddly enough, for a philosophical term, "supernatural existential" actually means what it appears to mean. It can be understood from its component parts: "Existential" denotes that it is a constituent of human existence – it distinguishes a human being from other kinds of beings. The "supernatural" tag we've already covered. It is something that transcends natural limitations. Put the two words together and we get a gifted feature of human existence, that is *not* an innate component of human nature. The supernatural existential shapes human nature, orienting it towards supernatural fulfillment (that's human being striving for absolute being, which is God). The supernatural existential is the reason we have the capacity to reach out to God. Another way to look at it is to think of the supernatural existential as the capacity we associate with human spirit. Our human spirit is open to God, and can transcend our human nature to reach out for God, because the supernatural existential gives our *being* this capacity. Our natural capacity won't get the job done; God's supernatural gift will.

There are several key things about the supernatural existential that are really important to our noticing quest. For starters, God's gift to humankind that orients us to God is universal. All humans – you and you and you and you and everyone – has received the capacity to transcend human nature and seek God. There is no if, and, or but in this equation; *everyone* means all of us. Another key thing is that our God-given orientation to God, and capacity to seek and receive God, untie the knotty paradox that binds Augustine's question. If the question is, "How can we search for what we do not already know?", the answer is that there is never a time in our conscious lives that we have not had an orientation to seek God. That leaves us with the second half of Augustine's query: how will we recognize God? We recognize God because human spirit recognizes God as our fulfillment. This is less tricky than it sounds. Remember that God is revealing exactly what we are seeking. God's revelation is God's self-disclosure. So, God reveals God, we are gifted with the openness to acknowledge and receive God, and to make the whole thing downright personal: God *addresses* his revelation to each and everyone of us (without exception). Cool, huh?

I haven't forgotten that our journey is a noticing quest. In fact, I've noticed that I have a noticing question for you: Have you ever noticed that the characters in fairy tales make bad choices? I mean it ... really bad choices. Here are two examples that have always bugged me. In *Goldilocks and the Three Bears*, the young Goldilocks is out and about in the woods and comes upon the house of the three bears. First things first: it is a bad decision for little girls to walk alone in the woods. I'd call it a classic "just say no" scenario. Nonetheless, as if one bad choice isn't enough, Goldilocks further decides to break into the bears' house and make herself at home. You know the story: she sleeps in their beds and eats their porridge. Not too smart, Goldilocks. A token search online would have told her that, in the last one hundred and twenty years, there have been one hundred and fifty-eight fatal bear attacks in North America. How could Goldilocks ignore this well-documented peril?

Similarly, anyone who has read the tragic account of Red Riding Hood knows that forests are worse than schoolyards. Forests contain wildlife, some of which are even larger threats than bears. You know what I'm talking about: I mean wolves. Tell me then, why would Red Riding Hood take a basket of food through the woods without an armed escort? Even when your mom says, "Time for a wander through the desolate woods to Grandma's," common sense needs to prevail.

When we tell youngsters both of these sorry tales, we often forget to mention why Goldilocks and Red Riding Hood made such bad choices. If these stories reflect human reality in any meaningful way, then there is only one honest answer. They made bad choices because they could. Let's tell it straight: humans of all sizes, hooded and unhooded, make bad choices because they can. Yes, we do have a God-given orientation

Goldilocks is free to
make bad choices

towards God, but that doesn't override our human freedom to reject God's self-disclosure. We have to take human freedom into account if we are going to make sense of our existential orientation to God. If we all have the capacity to recognize God's self-revelation, why aren't we better people on the whole? In Jesus, God's fullest self-disclosure to humankind, we see the love that God reveals. Yet, we also see evidence of divergent ways of responding. Some people make personal sacrifices to ensure the vulnerable are cared for, like Red Riding Hood. Other people violently trample over the innocent for personal gain, like the wolf who devoured Red's grandmother. We have all heard that God is present and is disclosing love. What gives? If we all have the capacity to tune into God's self-disclosure, why are some folks so tuned out?

Sometimes the dysfunction and cruelty in the world make us question God's presence. It's all too easy to mix up the issues of presence and response, yet we need to make a clear distinction. God's presence does not depend on us noticing God's constant presence. We see something of God's intention and character in the very fact that we are created with the capacity to notice God's continual offer. God desires to be present and desires that we notice so that we may respond. God *is* present and disclosed, but God is not an enforcer. God enables our orientation to the supernatural so that there is no barrier to accepting God's self-offer. No barrier, that is, other than ourselves.

Each of us is surrounded by pointers prompting us to notice God's continual offer, and we respond in greatly varying degrees. Some catch a glimpse and are intrigued, desire to notice more, and make that a conscious priority. Others catch a glimpse and form no clear idea whether noticing should be embraced or ignored. They fall into that passive fence-sitting mode between wonderment and bewilderment. Still others glimpse, make a hundred-and eighty-degree turn, and walk away. Rejecting God's offer is the prerogative of human freedom. As damaging as I believe this to be, it does not diminish God's offer of God's self to us all. Even for those who disregard the offer, God remains the reference point of all of their material and cognitive engagements. Regardless of whether we actively notice, or passively look away, God remains the horizon accompanying all human experience. Each of us can be plotted on a sliding scale of Red Riding Hood's to devious wolves. The same can be said about our varying degrees of consciously noticing, and consciously accepting or rejecting. Nevertheless, God's self-offer steadfastly remains open to us, and addressed to us.

Back in chapter three we touched on the symbolic function of language. Our words can represent things, but they can also misrepresent things. Misrepresentation is inevitably a risk we face when we talk about God. We want to communicate our thoughts well, but there is only so much we can say about divine mystery before our words run dry. If they don't, then we've got a false conception of mystery. On the other hand, sometimes words can delightfully draw in multiple meanings. In doing so, we gain understanding into the richness of certain words. For all the English teachers along on our journey, I'm not thinking about homonyms, though I know you love to mess with them. Things like: It's a human *right* to turn *right* at the lights. Or maybe: He plays in the *leaves* when his father *leaves* for work. Well, I could *type* homonyms all day, but they're really not my *type*. What I'm actually thinking about is that many of the themes we've covered can be expressed using a single word. This overarching word is *grace*.

We may have a host of different things in mind when we talk about "the grace of God." Yet whenever it is used, the word "grace" expresses a God-given gift. Grace is a gift that is present, intentionally given, and beneficial. To attribute something to the grace of God is to acknowledge a supernatural characteristic. Grace is a gift that transcends the capacity of human nature alone. Is it any wonder then that Rahner, and a host of other theologians, call God's self-disclosure grace? Putting this in even broader terms, we can say that God's self-communication is grace, *and* the gift of human orientation to God is grace. After all, when God gifted humankind with the capacity to notice divine revelation, God disclosed something of God's divine self. Similarly, because God's presence – whether it seems near or distant – reveals God, and God is continuously present, we all live in the presence of grace. God's presence is the reference point of all of our engagement with the world. We are continually engaging God's self-disclosure with every encountered thing, thought, and action. We live a graced existence, in God's presence, whether or not we tangibly feel that presence.

There is a lot more to this noticing business than meets the eye. Because even when it doesn't feel like God has met your eye (or ear, or heart, or mind), God is present. Through the highs and lows of this life, and the mystery we seek in the life to come, God is present. Rahner assessed this reality marvellously when he wrote:

> It is both terrible and comforting to dwell in the inconceivable nearness of God, and so to be loved by God himself that the first and last gift is infinity and inconceivability itself. But we have no choice. God is with us.[13]

Our everyday lives of graced existence can be overwhelming. Let's face it, we humans have control issues. We like to have a handle on the things that affect our lives, our livelihoods, and our relationships. God has no such handle. We simply cannot grasp God, and there is no manual or training course that can teach us how to handle the mystery of

God. Fortunately, God's self-disclosure is an invitation to engage divine mystery. Pointers, being what they are, give us points of entry. Our next step is to boldly go to where all real adventures must go … into the mystery.

5

Mystery

(or Discussing a Place Beyond Words)

When we get to the end of our journey and look back over the ground we've covered, this next bit will stick out in your mind. I can't help that – it's just the way it will be. I may as well get right to it, because there is no way to prepare you for what comes next. I need you to indulge me a wee bit. There is a statement that needs to be unleashed, and there's no sugar-coating it. Hang on to your hats, it very well might be the most profound statement I have ever shared. All set? You have been warned, here goes:

Scooby-Doo is the most theologically accurate portrayal of the Christian life in the history of television.

Just let that sink in for a moment - - - - *Scooby-Doo, Where Are You* simply nailed the day-to-day reality of Christian life. There is, of course, a big error in the overall Scooby template. We'll get to that after admiring the bigger thing that Scooby marvellously captures spot-on.

Here a brief refresher for those of you who haven't watched a Scooby-Doo cartoon in a while: Scooby-Doo travels with his pals Shaggy, Fred, Velma, and Daphne in a tricked-out van they call "the mystery machine." This, I think, is where the penny drops and your memories start flooding back: "*Aha, the mystery machine.*" You've got it! Scooby and the gang travel from town to town, from haunted house to enchanted amusement park, and engage – nay, *confront*, mystery. This is their everyday ongoing reality. Every episode finds Scooby-Doo in a new environment with a new cast of supporting characters (which almost always includes somebody's uncle). It doesn't matter where they travel or what backdrop castle, ranch, or theatre they visit; mystery is everywhere. In fact, mystery never takes a day off, and there isn't a blessed thing they can do about it. It's enough to make you wonder why they aren't certifiably crazy. Is this starting to sound like an insightful portrayal of the Christian life? And all along you thought Scooby-Doo was just a kid's cartoon.

The Christian life involves everyday engagement with divine mystery. It doesn't matter where we travel, who we visit, or even what clever name we have given our multi-colour van; divine mystery is ongoing. Some days, this everyday reality truly weighs on the Christian mind. In some big ways Scooby-Doo hits this nail right smack-dab on the head. The show certainly gets enough right to warrant a daytime Emmy award. At the very least they deserve the nod for *best van in a cartoon crime drama*. That said, there is one very important way in which Scooby-Doo is completely wrong, and utterly mistaken about our engagement with God. Scooby-Doo has a false sense of mystery. Scooby-Doo mystery is not *real* mystery at all. That, my friends, is likely why Scooby-Doo is marketed as a television show and not a theological dramatization of the Christian life. Sorry Scooby, you get a fistful of Scooby snacks for effort, but ultimately, your concept of mystery is so very far off the mark.

Mystery has had a makeover in recent years. Most of what passes for mystery in our twenty-first century culture isn't truly mystery. There are a massive number of movies, television shows, and novels with *murder mystery* and *unsolved mystery* themes. Each variant dresses up a basic template that relies heavily on interesting locations stocked with fetching hero characters. The trouble is that, like Scooby-Doo, the "mysteries" they tackle are all solvable. They aren't really mysteries at all; they're riddles. Once you notice this mystery makeover it becomes patently obvious. After all, if it's possible to "solve" an "unsolved mystery," then it's merely a riddle or conundrum. I can only assume that some Madison Avenue pollsters have determined that folks won't watch shows named *Resolving Conundrums* or *Puzzle Busters.* Instead we're offered mystery demoted to mere riddle, and that isn't going to help us with divine mystery.

When we seek the mystery of God, we engage divine mystery. None of us solve God like a riddle, nor do we solve divine mystery. Our lot is to live with mystery, engage mystery, and participate in mystery. If we are going to get our heads around divine mystery, we will need to retrieve an ancient understanding of it. The apostle Paul used the Greek word *mystērion*, which we translate as "mystery," quite a lot.[1] In his letter to the Christian community in Rome, Paul used mystery to describe God's unveiling of previously hidden knowledge. The mystery in question in Romans is that God's offer is addressed to Gentiles as well as Jews. This, Paul announced, was always God's intention (Romans 11). In his first letter to the Church in Corinth there is another great example of mystery unveiled. There, Paul said, "Listen, I will tell you a mystery! We will not all die, but we will all be changed" (1 Corinthians 15:51). Then Paul went on to share what God has revealed about resurrection.

These examples from Paul's letters offer great insight into the true character of mystery. God's mystery – the real deal mystery – can only be revealed by God. The content of God's revelation is God's self-disclosure, which reveals divine mystery. Hiddenness is in part revealed, though never exhausted. That is why an authentic portrayal of everyday Christian life can't sidestep or play down the centrality of divine mystery (Scooby and the gang take note). Christian life is lived seeking and engaging mystery, so that we may participate in mystery.

One of the ways that Christians acknowledge their participation in mystery is the celebration, or observance, of sacraments. This is exemplified by the various approaches to baptism, and communal observances of Jesus' last supper, we see across the spectrum of Christian traditions. Diverse language is used to describe these acts within the church. This often reflects the differing perceptions held in different traditions, and the elements of participation they choose to emphasise. Our concern is not with identifying the number of sacraments, or whether a church community "celebrates" a sacrament or "observes" an ordinance. Church rites, in all their communal expressions, are events that acknowledge God's love and presence. Sacraments are particularly significant to our pointer journey, because they incorporate visible signs and invisible presence.

To get to the heart of the classic characteristics of a sacrament, I will cede the floor to Peter Lombard (ca. 1100-1160). He is sometimes called Peter the Lombard, in reference to his roots in the Lombardy region of Northern Italy. Peter penned (or at least, quilled), what became the must-read standard four-volume theology textbook for aspiring medieval theologians. His scholarly definition of a sacrament draws on ideas that had been developing since the time of Augustine. Over to you, Peter:

> A sacrament is properly so called, which is a sign of the grace of God and the form of invisible grace, in as much as it bears the likeness of the grace and is its cause. Thus, the sacraments were instituted for the sake not only of signifying but of sanctifying mystery and sacrament.[2]

Thanks, Pete! This definition draws together some of the key ideas we've already encountered. Let's remember that a sign visibly signifies (points to) and symbolizes (as a representative presence) something that is not immediately visible. A sacrament is akin to this *except that it also communicates.* A sacrament involves a visible form that is aligned with the invisible presence of God's self-communication; which is grace.[3] In this light, we can easily imagine why the meeting of the physical presence and spiritual presence we affirm in baptism is called a sacrament. Here, as in the celebration of Communion – or the Lord's Table – God's presence and communicative grace resonate in our material being. This understanding of sacraments holds up, even if we view participation in the communion meal of bread and wine as a memorial remembrance of Jesus' last supper. Christians across traditions and epochs remember the words of Jesus: "Where two or three are gathered in my name, I am there among them" (Matthew 18:20). When our physical presence and spiritual presence are united in seeking and acknowledging Christ, we are met by the spiritual presence of Christ. Our orientation to God is, in essence, a sacramental orientation.[4]

By consciously drawing sacraments into our journey path, we find the idea of the sign and the signified is taken to a whole new level. As Peter Lombard said: "The sacraments were instituted for the sake not only of signifying but of sanctifying mystery and sacrament." The sanctifying (or righteously maturing) process of each and every Christian is rooted in their orientation to God. Our engagement of mystery is often an engagement with signifiers of mystery. God's mystery and our sacramental engagement with grace are truly worthy of our notice. When we actively notice God's constant offer, our sacramental orientation matures into a sacramental outlook – grace informs our being. This is vital because our lives are full of world-wobbling challenges that can hamper our journey.

Sacraments, and a conscious sacramental orientation, give us a place to plant our feet when mystery has us questioning our spiritual *terra firma*.

One of the beautiful aspects of participating in mystery is the opportunity to give language a rest. Talking about divine mystery is a tough business. It doesn't matter how much time you have to prepare, or how large your vocabulary is; talk about mystery and your words are doomed to fail. Apparently, mystery doesn't care about the small fortune you spent on elocution lessons. Mystery transcends language and brings out the stutter in all who try to harness it in a linguistic corral. If we're lucky our attempts can sound coolly cryptic or enigmatic, inscrutable or mystical. But what words can't do with mystery is exactly that thing words are supposed to do: we can't describe the essence of mystery. The funny thing is that we know when we have engaged mystery. We know when an experience transcends our ability to articulate the essence of that very same experience. So, what's a tongue to do? There aren't many options, it basically comes down to a single choice. We know we can't hit the bulls-eye, so we do our best to just hit the mystery dartboard. We find words to describe *something like* the mystery we cannot express. Sometimes we catch a glimpse of mystery by looking at its analogical reflection. This is a bit tricky and a few examples are definitely in order.

In the last chapter we noted that Augustine was concerned with the hows and whys of our orientation to God. Augustine was a Bishop in Roman North Africa, in the territory that is now Algeria. As would be expected, he had a deep concern for how the Christians in his region understood divine mystery. In particular, he wanted to help them envision the Holy Trinity of God the Father, Jesus (the Son sent by the Father), and the Holy Spirit (who was sent by the Father and the Son). Christianity is decisively monotheist; we acknowledge one God. Mysteriously, though God is One, God is a Holy Trinity of Father, Son, and Holy Spirit, with each enjoying a unique relation to the others. As odd as it sounds, when we talk about the Trinity, One is synonymous with Three (which is synonymous with One). This is not a take-it or leave-it proposition; it is a cornerstone of Christianity. The Trinity is so marvellous that we love God's divine mystery regardless of how thoroughly it provokes our intellect.

By now it should be clear that Augustine was a cerebral guy. He knew it was one thing for the human heart to seek the invisible God, but another thing altogether for the human mind to imagine the Holy Trinity. The heart may not need to visualize the Three-is-One Trinity, but the mind just can't help itself. Our intellects want to master knowledge even when mystery guarantees we've embarked on an absurd mission. Fortunately, Augustine trusted his heart but never abandoned his head. Nor did he expect others to engage mystery without rational contemplation. His challenge was nothing less than finding words to rationally describe the internal relationships which give the Holy Trinity its unique Three-is-Oneness. Augustine's answer was to offer six analogical comparisons that used describable relationships to represent a likeness of the Holy Trinity. One of these comparisons was a trinity of *Lover*, *Beloved*, and *Love*. Love is a condition that requires the presence of another – the *Beloved* object of one's love, and requires the feeling of *Love* that bonds the one that loves to the object that is loved. This analogy involves a triad of distinct things that interrelate in a unified way, which mimics relational hallmarks of the Holy Trinity. *Lover*, *Beloved*, and *Love* doesn't describe the essence of the mystery of the Holy Trinity. It is, however, an approachable word-picture of mystery, painted with analogy, likeness, and comparison. Augustine offered five more trinity analogies. If you read them all (in his rather tricky *De Trinitate*), you'll grasp enough from his comparisons to find new ways to engage the mystery of

God's Three-is-Oneness.

Using analogies to find words for divine mystery is more than simply a neat theological trick. Thomas Aquinas went so far as to say that our attempts to form knowledge of God are inescapably bound up in analogy. Thomas observed that each "perfection" (or absolute form of an attribute) in humankind is given by God. Humankind, in some manner, *shares* in attributes God defines and has given us. God has given and we have received, but humans and God are not alike in the way that two of the same species are alike. When it comes to being human, God is the principal cause of our being. What humankind and God have alike is being; we have being and God has being. That said, we are so obviously unlike God. To say that my neighbour Ed is good is quite different from saying God is good.[5] We cannot leap from our knowledge of Ed's goodness to a knowledge of God's goodness. Even though God is the cause of our being, the human attribute "good" and the divine attribute "good" are alike in name only. They are not equal to compare. They do not even have a generic likeness.

The bottom line is that, if we want to talk to each other about divine mystery, analogous language is really all we have. The single likeness we can leverage as a human reflection of God is our being: God has being, and thankfully, we have being. It's okay to acknowledge that our word-pictures of mystery will be painted with analogy, likeness, and comparison. This isn't necessarily a bad thing. Think about all of the analogies Jesus used to describe the Kingdom of God. Here's a classic example: "What is the kingdom of God like? And to what should I compare it? It is like a mustard seed that someone took and sowed in the garden; it grew and became a tree, and the birds of the air made nests in its branches" (Luke 13:18-19). There are great riches to be mined in the quarry of analogy.

There are likely some among our journeying cluster who think I've overstated this whole mystery business. I imagine that you're exasperatingly muttering: "Surely, we have the intellectual faculties to unravel mystery. After all, Sherlock Holmes could sniff the tobacco ash at the scene of a crime and deduce the tobacconist who sold it. That's pretty sharp considering that Holmes was only a fictional character ... and a Victorian with suspect taste in head-gear to boot!" Okay, I get your point. However, I need to push back a bit. I'm not suggesting that the good God-given intellect we all enjoy is deficient. No, our brains are just fine, but mystery is finer still. That's no slight on Sherlock, or the brains beneath his deerstalker cap. In fact, I think Sherlock can help us here. In Sir Arthur Conan Doyle's novel, *A Scandal in Bohemia*, there is a telling episode. As Dr. Watson narrates it, he is attempting to decipher a baffling letter that has arrived at Holmes' Baker street lodgings. Perplexed, Watson remarks to Holmes: "This is indeed a mystery. What do you imagine that it means?" Holmes, being no fellow's fool, replies: "I have no data yet. It is a capital mistake to theorize before one has data. Insensibly one begins to twist facts to suit theories, instead of theories to suit facts." Well said, Sherlock! Holmes remembered that hidden data must be unhidden before knowledge can be gained. Likewise, we must remember that our knowledge of God is hidden until God's self-disclosure unhides it. Even if we read our weight in daunting theological tomes, we cannot change the nature of mystery.

Yet again, it feels as if we have returned to where we started. We're back at square-one, face-to-face with mystery, and it's *still* mysterious. In actuality, we haven't returned; we never left. None of us are divine puzzle busters with a knack for resolving the *über*-conundrum we call mystery. Divine mystery is consistent, we are never ahead of it or behind it. When we are seeking God we are always, absolutely and unfailingly, facing mystery. Rest assured that, when we're facing mystery, we are in good company. I mean, we're all in on this together. Among the members of our facegod group I know I'll find you, and me, and everyone reading this, and Karl Rahner (yes, even Rahner). I know this because Rahner once wrote:

> ... we are always finding ourselves facing a mystery ... which is without limit, which grounds itself without having a ground, which is always there and always withdraws, intangible. We call it God.[6]

God is God. That's simply a way of saying that God is constant, and therefore constantly God. Because God in unchanging and ever-present, our earthly proximity to God never changes – each of us will live their entire life facing God.

If we take stock of where we are on our journey, the path so far has been a bit odd. We're keeping an eye open for pointers and increasing our noticing alertness, but some issues have crept up. God is hidden and mysterious, and the limitations of analogical language are hampering our problem-solving initiatives. Then there's that whole bit about problem-solving not working on mystery. Geesh! It's like we're stuck in the deepest mysterious silence trying to engage God. Hmmm ... yes, that is *exactly* where we are and what we're doing. Fortunately for us, silence *is* where we engage divine mystery; it is where we engage God ... and vice versa.

There is a lot to be gained in rethinking how we view hiddenness, because we don't *view* hiddenness at all. What would happen if we toss the idea of seeing what is hidden, and pay more attention to listening? The psalmists, the folks who wrote the five-book collection we call *Psalms*, grappled with hiddenness. When hiddenness felt like abandonment, one psalmist asked:

How long, O Lord? Will you forget me forever? How
long will you hide your face from me? (Psalm 13:1-2)

This feeling of distance weighed so heavily on another, that he
cried out:

I stretch out my hands to you; my soul thirsts for you like
a parched land. Answer me quickly, O Lord; my spirit
fails. Do not hide your face from me, or I shall be like
those who go down to the Pit. (Psalm 143:6-7)

Yet, for all of the anguish of feeling that God's face was hidden
– that God's active presence was absent – there always re-
mained the promise of hiddenness revealed:

For God alone my soul waits in silence; from him comes
my salvation.
He alone is my rock and my salvation, my fortress; I
shall never be shaken …
For God alone my soul waits in silence, for my hope is
from him. (Psalm 62:1-2, 5)

The silence of God's presence is a place of encounter. Where
better to encounter the mystery that transcends language than
in the silence that transcends language. We can catch glimpses
of the potency of silence in our human relationships. Have you
ever sat in a large waiting room where you are one of only two
people waiting? If you have ever sat at a departure gate in an
airport with only one other person, you know exactly what I'm
getting at. It doesn't matter if the other person sits out of view
or thirty feet away, you can feel their presence in the silence.
    The presence of a truly close friend can speak with knowing
intensity. Old married couples are fountains of this type of
silent communication. I'm talking about the kind of couples

who finish each other's sentences, and know what each other is thinking with just a glance. There is a beautiful wordless presence between those who share the deepest bonds of friendship, trust, and love. There is richness in their silence; a presence and intimacy that transcends words. Now, if that is the case between people, imagine the possibilities of God's silence.

Rahner wrote some of the most beautiful and questioning prayers I know of. A collection of his prayers from his early years as a Jesuit Priest was published under the telling title, *Encounters with Silence.* Rahner's prayers profoundly exhibit the liberation, expectation, and weight that accompanied his recognition of living before God. In his heartfelt words an equilibrium of personal investment and humble acceptance coexist. Rahner's prayers, and his broader theological writing, consistently emphasised that Christians cannot be passive. God's silence must be engaged; we must *listen* if we desire to *hear* and encounter divine mystery. Of course, most of us have little patience for the discipline of engaging silence. Aware of this (being decidedly human himself), Rahner offered this advice in a piece titled *The Answer to Silence*:

> Wait, listen without expecting any unusual experience … Bear with yourself. You will discover how everything that emerges in such silence is surrounded by an indefinable distance, permeated as it were by something that resembles a void. Do not yet call it God! It is only what points to God and, by its namelessness and limitlessness intimates to us that God is something other than one more thing added to those we usually have to deal with. It makes us aware of God's presence, if we are still and do not flee in terror from the mystery which is present and prevails in the silence ….[7]

The distinction Rahner makes between God, and the silent prompts that point to God, is extraordinarily important. Pointers come in all shapes and sizes, and permeate all of our cognitive experiences. We notice them and they make us aware of our orientation to God. Still, with all this going for them, pointers offer no short-cuts *around* silent mystery to God. There is no spiritual bypass to save wear and tear on our spiritual tires. Pointers may point us to a space or posture in which we listen to hear God, but our conscious attention to listening is *almost* always down to us. Almost? Well, yes … almost always, because sometimes silence inhabits noise.

No discussion about seeking in silence is complete without an acknowledgement that GOD CAN BE REALLY LOUD. God may speak as a still small voice but God also has some powerful lungs – God can seriously belt it out (yes, I'm leaning pretty hard on anthropomorphic likeness-language here). The Old Testament contains various examples of temporary manifestations of the presence and glory of God. These are known as *theophanies*, a term which combines the Greek words for *God* and *appearance*. While theophanies are named for their visual element, they can also be plenty loud. How loud? Well, loud like thunder (Exodus 19:16), or the crackling of a consuming fire (Leviticus 9:24), or the sound of trumpets that signify the presence of God (Exodus 19:16, 19; Psalm 47:5). It is all right and good to quote the directive to "be still and know that I am God" (Psalm 46:10); just remember that stillness isn't always met with silence. I don't want anyone to get the impression that we only encounter God in quiet contemplation. We encounter God any way that God desires to reveal God's self.

Divine mystery is something we can safely assume will be mysterious. That's really about all we can say, other than, we know what mystery is *not*. We know the unknowable is *not* knowable – that mystery transcends knowledge. On first glance that may not seem particularly helpful. Think again, because there is a meaningful theological tradition that flows from embracing that God is uniquely "unknowable." God is acknowledged to be above all known things, and therefore better known by this unique distinction than by comparisons to what we can know. Whether we subscribe to this approach or not, it effectively emphasises our need for humility when seeking God. There is a quote I have framed on my desk to remind me that encountering God is quite different than "knowing" God. Until God's hiddenness is revealed, the mystery we seek will remain mystery. The quote is from an article by (you guessed it) Karl Rahner. It reads:

> The supreme knowledge which man has of God is to know that he does not know God, insofar as he knows that what God is surpasses all that we can understand of God ... the climax of our knowledge of God is knowledge of our ignorance.[8]

If you're curious enough to flip this framed quote over, you'll find another that reads:

> The mystery of God remains. That is of the essence of theology. It is not the unmasking of a secret, allowing it to become self-evident, but a glimpse into the bright obscurity of the divine mysteries ....[9]

Yep, that's more Rahner. I highly recommend finding time to peruse his writings. And if you find some extra time, feel free to pass it on to me. Of course, the question remains whether we really can find time if we haven't lost it first. Curious, isn't it? Year after year we seldom give time a second of thought or a minute of reflection. Yet, isn't there something of "the bright obscurity of the divine mysteries" to be glimpsed in time?

Before we gear down the mystery machine leg of our journey, let's make time to consider the importance of noticing time.

Here's a little fact that almost never comes up in conversation: I am more than just a pointing-accomplice on our noticing trek, I'm also the third cousin of Herbert George Wells (1866–1946).[10] You probably know him better by his pen name, H. G. Wells. His family called him Bertie, but I missed him by some seventeen years and seventy-one hundred kilometers, so I've never called him anything. Among his truly prodigious output, Wells wrote a novella called *The Time Machine*. It popularized the much used and abused Sci-Fi time travel sub-genre. Time travelling adventures are fascinating because the characters are singularly hung up on leaving the present. It never seems to occur to them that they can stay where they are in time and still be connected to all of time *and eternity*. Yes, I really wrote that … all in favour of a little time travelling detour, read on.

Let's go back in time to make sense of our present time. What is time? This is a slippery question. Augustine wrote that, "We do in fact understand 'time' when we talk of it, and we also understand when we hear someone else talking of it … If nobody's asking me, I know. If I'm trying to explain it to someone who asks me, I don't know."[11] Augustine had some very abstract ideas about time. More importantly, for our journey, he also had a very clear idea about eternity. For Augustine, eternity is always present as the *other* that eludes humankind. It is the counterpoint to our experience of present-time. Eternity is that thing beyond time that continuously informs us that the mystery of God exceeds our imagination, and the majesty of God is beyond our comprehension.[12]

Bringing eternity into the picture helps us in a roundabout way. We glimpse time like we glimpse God, by the attributes we dimly perceive and by negation. We know what time *is not*. Time is not eternity. All of us have a biological conception and a birth that initiates and animates our being in the world. Because we have a beginning, we know that no human can be eternal. We all-too clearly understand that we're time-bound. There are other comparisons that also aid our insight. Here's an engagement comparison: God's eternity is mystery and God's omnipresence (ever-presence) is mystery. Just as we engage God's mystery, we also engage time. Simply being "in" time means that we participate in time, including time's relation to eternity and the promise it holds.

We have seen that wherever we engage, we encounter. This provides another comparison: We encounter God in sacrament and via our sacramental orientation (which seeks God's presence). Similarly, we encounter eternity in time.[13] Just as God, being omnipresent, is always in absolute proximity to us, eternity is in absolute proximity to time. We experience time as an ongoing succession of fleeting *now* moments. This is contrasted by eternity, which is indivisibly *always*. Because eternity is without the beginning and end boundaries of time, eternity overlaps all our *now* moments.[14] All of our time moments have an equal proximity to eternity. This is particularly cool, because our equal human proximity to God's eternity – across all time – means we *all* share a single proximity to God regardless of where we are in time. This is big! The time of the church fathers, and (in their time) the church fathers themselves, have the same proximity to God in eternity that we do! Our journey in time is, in this sense, really *our* collective journey. The whole of humankind share time and, with this, the whole of the Church is connected by shared time and common proximity across all centuries. When we notice God's continuous self-offer, we are noticing the same offer that has been addressed to all humankind regardless of era.

There is an equality to time that we cannot upset, control, or manipulate. It may seem absurd, but history amply displays our obvious desire to master time. If not, why would we invent instant coffee, instant mashed potatoes, or microwave ovens? These are things that aim to tame and corral time for their own devious purposes. If you don't think instant coffee is devious, you must be drinking some miracle brand I haven't tried yet. It still boggles the mind that we would try to simplify a process that only requires two ingredients: coffee and water. Instant coffee isn't really about simplification, it's about having our way with time. Time, of course, is having none of this. It favours a slow drip and sneers at our freeze-dried *instant* nonsense.

Let's cap off our foray into mystery and time by adopting our own twist on Scooby-Doo's Mystery Machine van. We'll call our ride the Noticing Utility Vehicle (or "NUV" if you're a serious vehicular gearhead). This will give us a convenient way to stick together in time as we engage and encounter divine mystery. We won't even argue over the time setting on the dashboard clock. We know that all human time exists in reference to God in eternity. That's right: Time is a pointer too! All moments "in" time point to the eternity that defines time, just as all material, cognitive, and experiential pointers point to the eternal God that defines them.

So, does EVERYTHING point to God? Does EVERYTHING exist in reference to God? Does EVERYTHING that points to and references God reveal the CONSTANT OFFER OF GOD? Maybe my trashy garbage bin story seems a little less odd now. Maybe your own *noticing that you noticed* story is making a bit more sense now.

Eureka! What do we do now? How do we engage and en-counter amidst the sea of pointers that are flooding into view? Strap into our Noticing Utility Vehicle; we're five chapters in and we've got five chapters remaining in our journey. We've been rambling through the ethereal thickets of pointing, presence and mystery. Now it's time to bring it all down to earth. Let's get practical.

We'll call our ride the
Noticing Utility Vehicle

Part Two

Participating

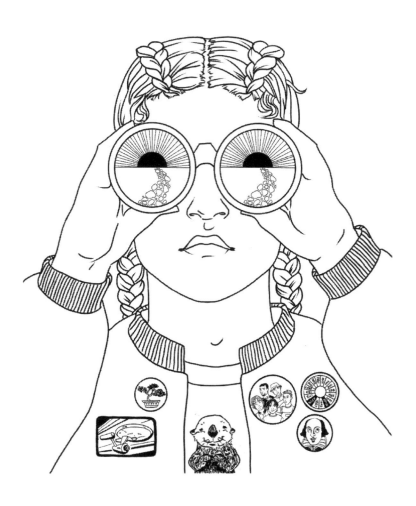

6

Secular Stuff
(and Sacred Space)

Upon reflection, Hamlet, "To be or not to be" isn't the question. No one who has ever uttered this oft-quoted question, has ever really had an option. None of us asked to *be*. It's not as if some are born *to be*, some achieve *be*ness, and some have *be*ness thrust upon them (no malevolence intended, Malvolio). The whole *be* question has pretty much been settled before Hamlet asks for our input. We *be*. If I may deign to correct a Dane, the burning question isn't *whether* to be, but rather, *how* to be. This *how* question takes on a fresh dimension for all who notice God, notice that they have noticed God, and then seek to consciously engage with God. After all, we need to do some heartfelt noticing before we self-identify as Christian. Now, if you're sore about my blatant abuse of Shakespeare, don't feel you need to take my word on this. Let's bring in a random stranger to describe the fallout of conscious noticing. I know, let's listen in to some real-life comments made by Bruce Cockburn. Bruce often says smart things (apparently kicking at the darkness helps the light go on upstairs).

I'll set the scene: Bruce Cockburn is a Canadian musician. Cockburn can be heard on dozens of albums and seen on a Canadian postage stamp. He was observed and celebrated in the 2013 documentary film *Pacing the Cage*. If you are not familiar with Cockburn, I invite you to put this book down immediately and check him out online. Its alright with me if it takes you a while to come back. Don't worry about missing anything. I'll wait ....

...

... Good to have you back. If you watch *Pacing the Cage*, you'll hear Cockburn offering up a rather personal story. Musing on his milestone 1973 song, "All the Diamonds in the World," Cockburn revealed: "For me 'All the Diamonds' was a turning point. It's a record of the moment when I decided that I was, in fact, a Christian. It seemed clear to me that there was such a thing as a spiritual reality; an extra something that deserved to be paid attention to. And I spent a long time trying to figure out the best way to pay attention to it. And I guess I'm still doing that."

Cockburn's comments capture a unique moment of conscious noticing. I certainly relate to his *aha* moment, and suspect that many of you do as well. In every life there are potent moments when noticing emerges from the cloak of unconscious interaction. It's like something has gradually moved from the corner of your eye, until it is unmistakeably confronting you front-and-center. This kind of noticing cuts right to the core of our identity. Once this happens there is no such thing as *unnoticing*. So, having consciously noticed the constant offer of God – that "extra something" accompanying our lives – there is a need to figure out how to pay attention to God. I particularly appreciate Cockburn's remarks because he doesn't present the reality of noticing as a fleeting event. Noticing, and figuring out the best way to pay attention, are ongoing aspects of responding. Noticing and figuring out are engagement activities. Noticing is never passive, because noticing kick-starts participation. Once noticing has captured our attention, we begin the ongoing task of figuring out what our participation will look like. Our desire and intellect just seem to naturally intertwine and set a course for participation.

With time, these woven strands become increasingly recognizable as the very fabric of life.

Mapping out how we participate in our noticing reality is not for the faint of heart. It's a tricky undertaking and our understanding of it changes along with our understanding of God's offer. There is an ebb and flow to every noticing quest. Noticing informs our orientation to God, which in turn informs our orientation to noticing. With so many moving parts, it's comforting to know that some aspects don't ever change. If we notice the constant offer of God, we're also going to notice that we live before God, and in the presence of God. That never changes. There is a stability in the ebb and flow. As we've seen, everything, everyone, and all time exists in reference to God. Reassuringly, these things are stable and ongoing too. All change considered, what changes most is *us*. Noticing and embracing the constant offer of God raises *a lot* of questions. Sure, there are a few easy questions that shouldn't slip us up too much. But there are plenty of big ones, like how will noticing affect my interaction with God, and people, and places, and culture, and material stuff. Our changes in orientation *are* going to shape how we, individually and collectively, handle our interactions. The *handling* that each of us needs to sort through, is precisely what I mean when I use the term *participation*.

Further down the line we'll consider interactions with space and God and people. Right now, let's start by dealing with all the junk we have lying around. We are mavens of matter, aficionados of acquisition, and far too often, connoisseurs of crap. We've got stuff in our homes, in our garages, in our storage sheds, in our parents' basements, in our lockers at work, and in the trunks of our cars. Whoa, do we have stuff. We've even got *double-stuff* in our Oreo cookies. If we desire to be nimble noticers, what should our relationship with our stuff be? How do we decide which is the good stuff (that maybe even God likes), and which is the bad stuff (that we shouldn't sell off at a church fundraiser)? If only we could shop at stores that are clearly marked as "Christian," and buy stuff that is clearly labelled "for Christians." Wait a second, I think I saw a store just like that in the outlet mall next to the highway. You have probably seen a store just like it. The names given to such stores, and the branding on their products, merge Christian culture and consumer culture. If material interaction is our question, is this the answer?

The production and consumption of goods that are intentionally aligned with faith is not a new phenomenon. In North America, this has been an element of the Christian cultural experience since the late 1700's.[1] The modern Christian marketplace was founded on the Christian bookstore retail niche. Christian bookstores began dotting the retail landscape in the 1950's, and a national presence was well established in America by the early 1970's. Initially non-Christians were the target consumers. Proprietors operated with an outward looking orientation. Their focus was to use their businesses as channels for Christian witness.[2] In 1978, 68% of sales within the niche were generated by books, including a lot of Bibles.[3]

A Christian Booksellers trade association was founded in 1950.[4] Their growth in membership paralleled the expansion of the Christian goods market. In 1965 the association included 725 member stores. By 1975 this figure had more than doubled to 1850 stores. This ballooned to 3200 members operating 4000 stores by the end of 1984. Even though my math skills are largely the result of playing with number-shaped fridge magnets as a kid, I know these figures mean something. "Christian stores" morphed from niche bookstores into mainstream specialty stores. In 1995 the Christian retail sector in the United States alone comprised over 7000 locations.[5] Sales that year were estimated at around three billion dollars.[6] In the current millennia the Christian market has fragmented into a mix of retail stores, catalogue marketing, and online e-tailers. As I write this, the largest of the web and catalogue companies offers customers more than 300,000 "Christian products."[7] Okay, that's enough numbers; I'll put the fridge magnets away now.

Christian bookstores have become marketplaces that specifically target Christian consumers. This is where things get a bit weird. These stores now sell books, music, clothing, jewelry, greeting cards, bumper stickers, mass produced art, novelty items, and more. Manufacturers and wholesalers offer these stores a mind-boggling array of Christianized gift items to stock. Some are cutesy, some are sincere, and all are consumer goods. Inescapably we have to call this what it really is: an industry that feeds religious material consumption. It is fueled by Christian-themed marketing that, in many cases, is masterminded by prominent consumer goods companies.

Marketers understand that visual imagery plays an important role in Christian culture. It is a culture in which theology and symbolism are inextricably mixed. Commercial interests are not shy about exploiting this connection. Images such as the *ichthus* fish, the crucifixion cross, and renderings of the lamb of God frequently adorn Christian products. Symbols become a vehicle to augment everyday items with a feel-good Christian twist. How about that? Clever marketing folks are branding material pointers so we'll see that they exist in reference to God. Hmm … perhaps, but I suspect that most are chiefly concerned with attracting purchasers. I try not to get too cynical when I see Mary and Joseph salt and pepper shakers, but it's not easy.

Before we steer things back onto the pointer path, there is a textbook case of marketing weirdness we can't pass by. Formally, this marketing mayhem is known as Christian copycatting. Copycatting is the practice of making like or identical versions of existing products. The Christian copycat market is comprised of religious themed versions of products that have achieved success in the broader "secular" market. Where proprietary rights prevent close copying, there's an emphasis on coat-tail offerings like Christian accessories. Perhaps you've seen the *Guitar Praise* repackaging of the established Guitar Hero and Rock Band game franchises, or the "Jesus the Good Shepherd" iPhone case.[8] The breadth of copycat products is vast, and their similarities with secular products are intentionally blatant. Skye Jethani is a podcaster and pastor who has studied Christian copycat marketing. Jethani's assessment of the phenomenon is not flattering: "With a speed matched only by the Chinese black market, Christian merchandisers produce knockoffs of every secular phenomenon virtually overnight."[9] At best we can award these enterprises with high marks for efficiency, varying marks for ethics, and their marks for originality … well, let's just say they're somewhat off the mark. There is a fine line between targeted promotion and cultural exploitation. Christianity is not a commodity and God is not a product. Applying words and images associated with Christianity onto products and packaging is a high-risk marketing strategy. Even when done with the finest intentions, it looks a lot like commodification.

I don't want to give the impression that I'm down on the folks who sell this stuff. Let's face it, you're holding a book that is, in essence, a Christian targeted product. I'm well aware that I'm a Christian author who, for the most part, sells books to other Christians. I get that retailers are sellers, and sellers sell stuff. As far as consumer products go, I'm not even overly concerned about whether a nativity egg timer is frivolous, or beneath the treasured narratives of the birth of Jesus in a stable. If you feel the need to integrate a reminder of Christ's humble birth into your kitchen environment, do what you gotta do. However, we can draw the line when marketers try to elevate their manufactured "Christian" pointers over supposedly iffy "secular" pointers. You know, when they imply that the Bibleopoly board game is somehow better than the Monopoly game you already own. That's right, just because Bibleopoly "combines the fun of a property trading game with the remarkable cities of the bible," doesn't mean it's a spiritually enriched pointer.[10] If every thing points to God, then regardless of packaging, EVERYTHING points to God.

What can we take away from the weirdness of branding consumer products as if they're somehow differentiated Christian things? I suggest that if this teaches us anything, it's that our material stuff question is actually a lot bigger than our mountainous piles of stuff. Our exploration into interaction with material goods is really about questioning the boundaries we've placed around the terms *sacred* and *secular*. As long as we're in noticing mode, let's take some time to rethink what we're really saying when we use these terms as labels. This is so much bigger than labelling consumer products. We use sacred and secular to label activities and ideas as well.

Let's apply our pointer principle to the problem: Everything, including the best and the worst products, ideas, and activities, exist as pointers referencing God. On the material front, there are a lot of just plain bad products in the world. Remember though, that it is only in relation to *good* that we know that bad is *not good*. The label "secular" has become a loaded word that somehow has come to imply *distant from God*. Does this suggest that secular denotes a sphere in our world where the Holy Spirit cannot work? Are secular entities things that disengage human spirit, by somehow preventing human spirit from reaching out beyond? Is secular a fancy way of saying *off-limits for pointers*? Let's drop by a commonplace setting packed with secular references and see if we can make sense of this. Come along and join me in a seventh inning stretch … *Take Me Out to the Ball Game*!

Okay, we're at the baseball park. The park is a swell piece of land encircled by an ingeniously engineered building (momentarily forgetting Fenway's green monster). The field, the building, the rules, and the equipment, are not overtly or specifically fashioned for practices associated with religion; by this definition they are secular. Heck, baseball is the national pastime of a country that has constitutionally enshrined its secularity.[11] It's grand slam secular! Okay, now what exactly does that mean? Let's break down the secular pieces:

The playing field is land. In some places they put a carpet on it, but it's still land. You hardly need me to point out the connection between God and the land given to God's people. What we sometimes forget is that all land is holy land. No disrespect intended to those who hold rather tightly to Palestine, but God's gift of land to humankind (let's call it "Earth") is all holy land. Creation points to God, even when it's a playing field with four bases and a modest molehill.

The building around the playing field is a showcase of God-given human intellect. It's the architectural answer to the long-asked question: what must I build to sell six-dollar hot dogs and four-dollar bottles of water? The complexities of a baseball stadium are posterchildren for cognitive pointing.

The rules of baseball are a thinly veiled excuse for human interaction. At its heart, every act of human interaction is one human being reminding another human being of references to God. It is impossible for created humankind to interact without reference to their Creator. Interactively live, laugh, love, and play ball – whatever your position, baseball rules point to the God of peace and community.

The equipment used to play baseball is shockingly simple for a national pastime. The participants only need a ball, a stick, and a glove. Organized leagues are fond of using little rubber foot-pillows they call bases, but a lack of pillows never stopped a sandlot game. In my schoolyard days, I remember sharing a few gloves and not caring much about catching bare-handed. The simplicity of baseball equipment is like a recipe for inclusion. Aside from the obvious material and cognitive pointer-tude of baseball equipment, it also mirrors the universal nature of God's continual offer. God doesn't care how you're equipped; everyone receives an offer to participate (even me, and I make up dubious words like "pointer-tude").

Setting frivolity and my unashamed pointer-tudeness aside, we see that it is absurd to try to separate secular baseball from its references to God. Do we consciously notice these references every time we go to the ballpark? No, but we are apprehending and engaging God whether or not we *consciously* recognize it. This should give us pause to think before we derisively write anything off as *secular*. Human spirit is still reaching in secular interactions. The Holy Spirit is active the world-over, unhampered by barriers separating secular and sacred settings. For some this whole exercise may seem overblown, but too many of us have been culturally conditioned to hide God in church. When it comes to sacred and secular, noticing God's presence will make us notice our personal biases. Rahner observed that, "If we want to get rid of the impression of a secular world, in which there is nothing like a Holy Spirit, then we shall have to stop looking for him only under explicitly religious labels of the kind to which our religious training has accustomed us."[12] Good call, Karl! Our participation in the secular world is not an abandonment of the sacred world. When our relationship to our stuff is governed by our noticing orientation to God, we gain the insight to separate the beneficial material pointers from the distracting ones.

Discerning readers in our journeying group will have noticed the vintage of my story references. I'll fess up, I'm a baby boomer. Actually, I need to be more specific: I reckon that I'm the very last baby boomer. The date parameters for the boomer generation tend to vary from source to source. No one seems really sure when it ended. No one, that is, but me. I'm very sure that I was born on the last day of the last month of the last year of boomerdom. I am, my friends, the last boomer. I share, along with the boomers born just before me, a special fondness for the Apollo 11 moon landing. In the summer of '69 we were just the right age to be enthralled by the command module and the lunar rover.[13] The astronauts seemed pretty cool, too. The whole mission was a really big deal. Space was a really big deal. Looking back, I think this was because the astronauts in space had *a lot* of space … I mean personal space. Seriously, for a little while Neil Armstrong got a whole planet all to himself. Me, I had to share a bedroom with my older brother. Having to share space with your brother is a life shaping experience. I guess that's why I always thought there was good space (like a private planet), and suspect space (like a small room with bunkbeds). I got over the trauma of sharing a bedroom with my brother, but I never got over my fascination with space. When I finally noticed that I was noticing things, I made a point of noticing a few things about space.

Space isn't as far away as it looks in NASA documentaries. It's everywhere and all around all of us. Do you know anyone who doesn't occupy a physical space? Neither do I. Some folks seem to have no concept of personal space, but we all have it. I'm not a physicist, so I can't quantify my space theories. However, a lifetime of anecdotal evidence suggests that there are three unimpeachable space facts: We all take up space, we all value space, and we all make value judgements about space. There are spaces that we think are swell (like that 52 flavours ice cream joint), and spaces we're leery of (like those shack offices on used car lots). In much the same way that we culturally herd material goods, activities, and ideas into separate secular and sacred silos, we categorize and label space.

Try closing your eyes and envisioning a sacred space in your life. - - - - If your mind pictured something, ask yourself why that space seems sacred to you. It's not always easy to identify why one space feels different than another. There are places, like the interior of a cathedral or a favourite room to pray in, that instinctively feel like spaces for engaging God. Other places, like a cemetery or a secluded lake, feel sacred in a difference sense. They awaken feelings for a loved one, or stir a tranquil and uplifting memory. Some places are considered sacred because they have been consecrated for use by a church community. They are intentionally set aside for community rituals like marriage, or sacraments like communion and baptism. God is openly invited into spaces like these. Visiting a church sanctuary or a church camp, we may find ourselves predisposed to open up to God's presence. There are cultural and emotional factors that make us tend towards openness in some spaces. Space can make us comfortable, worshipful, and prompt our conscious seeking of God. All of this is good, but it also raises a tough question: if we're favouring certain places to consciously seek God, are we short-changing all the other spaces in which God is consciously seeking us?

God's continuous self-offer is never absent from our space. There is no border wall that is keeping God out of the spaces we have forgotten to call sacred, or limiting God to the spaces we do call sacred. It's folly to string velvet rope to distinguish a sacred red carpet from a secular one. Sacred space isn't in our real estate portfolio; we don't get to decide what to list as sacred. I am conscious that when I close my eyes and think about sacred space, I fall way short of the mark. I have to remind myself that my personal favourite spaces do not define sacred space. It is God's presence that defines sacred space.

One of the amazing things about our noticing journey is that we're running into God's presence at every turn. No matter what topic we're exploring, we eventually bore through the surface and find presence at the core. In candy terms, God's presence is like the Tootsie Roll center of a Tootsie Pop lolly. If we're patient and stick with any noticing topic long enough, we'll find presence is the heart of the matter. Presence and revelation go hand-in-hand. Wherever and however we encounter God's revelation, whether internally or externally, we are invited to notice God's presence. This reality is the same front-to-back as it is back-to-front: Wherever and however we encounter God's presence, we are invited to notice God's revelatory offer of self. There is no space in which conscious noticing will miss the mark. God's presence is such an incredibly large target (otherwise known as *everywhere*), that space itself points to God. Space exists in reference to God.

I appreciate everyone in our journeying group, but for a moment I'm going to single out those who have been fighting the urge to curse at me (or unleash a sternly worded tweet). Let's get this bubbling tension out of the way. If you fought off muttering "Of course God is present in baseball diamonds," a few pages ago, take a moment to robustly mutter now. Great. We're all friends here, even if you resort to some healthy muttering. Sometimes we have to say the obvious to check whether we're all on the same page. Yes, God is present at baseball games (and maybe God occasionally helps the Angels stretch a single into a double). I also concede that the concept of divine presence at Wrigley Field was openly debated during the Chicago Cub's 107-year championship drought. What I said at the top of this chapter, Cubbies fans have known for decades: mapping out how we participate in our noticing reality is not for the faint of heart.

God's self is offered, like all lesser offers, to be noticed and to engage our participation. This seems clear enough. At first glance, though, the idea of participating in God's space may seem oddly foreign. How can we participate in space? I propose that the answer doesn't involve a giant leap for humankind. This mission involves a simple approach, quite unlike a lunar approach. We participate in space by consciously engaging God in whatever space we are in. With space, it's never a matter of "you can't get there from here." You are always already in the space that points to God, so why not find some interesting ways to acknowledge it? Here are two examples of conscious participation and engagement. As with all participation endeavours, you set the tone. If one of these examples outwardly appears more *sacred* than the other, don't worry. I'd bet my bottom dollar that your intention while participating will be obvious to God, who is sharing space with you. It could just be that secular is in the heart of the beholder, and sacred is in the eye of the noticer.

For the first example we're going to revisit the Eastern Orthodox use of icons. One of the beautiful things about this tradition is that the display of icons is not limited to the wonderfully intentional architecture of Orthodox churches. Icons are also displayed in other spaces, like offices and homes. The practice of displaying icons in the home carries on an ancient tradition. In the first-century there were no dedicated church buildings. Christians would gather to worship in private homes, where there would quite naturally be an altar. Continuing this, icons are now displayed in homes to serve as altars. In a home this space is generally referred to as the *icon corner* (or the red corner). The icons often have special display shelves, and are traditionally placed facing east. In our exploration of icons and the value of symbols, we saw that icons have historically attracted both advocates and opponents. Not everyone is attracted to icons and not everyone is comfortable with establishing an altar in their home. For our purposes, the traditional pro and con arguments do not apply – we're focused on the sacredness of space. What I appreciate about icons in the home is that their visual presence is an acknowledgement of God's presence. An icon corner doesn't move around the house when you redecorate. No, its place is set as the spiritual center of the home. An icon corner is a profound reminder that we live in God's space, and that God is present in our most intimate space – our home.

The second example of participating in space is kind of kooky. There are crafty people who do decorative things with yarn and space ... on a very large scale. This wild and woolly form of expression is called *yarn bombing,* which makes the folks who participate *yarn bombers.* Yarn bombers create art installations by augmenting everyday things with yarn. Picture a statue or a tree covered (and usually beautified) with a colourful sleeve of yarn. It's akin to public graffiti, except that there is no malicious intent. Bombers have a code: they may cover a street sign, but they don't mess with the visibility or readability of the sign. This distances them from charges of vandalism. Responsible yarn bombers also know when it's time to remove their installation. This is a good thing because some installations are super big. Teams of bombers have been known to cover buses, buildings, and even city squares. On one hand, you might say this is subversive activity. Emerging artforms have a long history of being shellacked with the subversive brush (and much worse). However, when it is responsibly applied and removed, yarnbombing can be a beautiful thing.

So how does yarnbombing fit in with our noticing quest? Ideologically, there are several strong parallels. I like it that the knitters, crocheters, and fibre artists, who engage in yarn bombing, have advanced noticing skills. They have to because they're seeking out interesting public space to decorate. Along with this, I see that something theologically significant is in play. Yarn bombing is about intentionally giving *unusual* attention to *very usual* spaces. This is where the yarn bombing mindset aligns with the desire to consciously notice and intentionally participate in space. This is why it can be a beautiful and visual public prayer in yarn. Noticing and yarn-celebrating God's space can be participation informed by intention. Think of it as an opportunity to prettify pointers to presence.

Icons in the home and art in the public square are examples of visual interactions that prompt space participation. Visuals are tools of acknowledgement, but there are plenty of other acknowledgement options. We can bunch together and consciously sing Christmas carols in door-to-door space. We can silently pray while sitting in a parking space. You can stop this very moment and seek God in your reading space. The choices are endless but the intention remains constant: noticing the constant offer of God revealed in God's presence.

Weaving our way through stuff and space has opened up noticing possibilities. We can see that the division between secular and sacred is not carved in stone. It is fashioned by our orientation to God and the intent we bring to our everyday noticing. Noticing pointers, and seeking God's presence as the matter-of-fact way we live, fosters a sacramental outlook. When we participate in a sacrament, we seek and *anticipate* God's presence. Likewise, when we intentionally seek to participate in the reality of God's everyday presence, we do so with a sense of anticipation. Whether held softly or voiced loudly, anticipation is a key ingredient. We each tailor our own approach to participation. Our group journey will, no doubt, generate diverse personal experiences. Readers will develop their own ideas about anticipation, and its place within a sacramental outlook. Before we move on to our next topic, I'll share my thoughts. My approach to participation is grounded in an understanding that *anticipation is not expectation.*

You can stop this very moment and
seek God in your reading space

No one will venture to seek for very long if they don't occasionally find. One of the ways I avoid noticing burn out is to remind myself what it is I anticipate finding. I never expect that an ecstatic mountaintop experience is just around the next bend. It isn't sky-parting bells and whistles and tongues of fire that I anticipate finding. No, that's miles away from what I seek and anticipate. If I am open and patient, I anticipate noticing that I am an addressee of God's grace. I notice that God is present and I am a recipient of God's self-offer. I understand this as an invitation to participate in God's grace. The noticing that we have been investigating is all about orientation and awareness of our relation to God. The core of this relation is God's grace. God's grace is the pinnacle of humanly divine encounter. Grace is the noticing big-splash high diving board that towers above the low boards of lesser splashes. Think my metaphors are all wet? There's only one way to know for sure: Turn the page, we're taking a deep dive into grace!

7

Grace
(of God, Agents, and Otters)

As journeys go, ours could be classified as risky behaviour. Although it began as a simple trash talk pointer tale, this expedition has taken on a life of its own. We've been through time and space and we're still going. Having kicked things off with my eureka trash bin, I do feel somewhat responsible for the toll my tale has taken. How can I make it up to you? After all we've been through, how can I stay in your good graces? Whoa ... hold the phone while my head does a double-take. What's this about staying in *good graces*? I've tossed this phase around many times, but this time it seems to have boomeranged back on me ... duck! What the heck are "good graces"? Just when you thought we might be hitting an easy stretch on the notice-quest path, we've got to sort out good graces.

When in doubt, make a list. I'll jot down some of the graces I know and we'll consider whether they are any good. Let's start with Grace Kelly. This Grace was featured in a slew of Hollywood films before retiring at the age of 26. What in the world would make a super successful film star retire in their mid-twenties? I guess she got a better offer ... jumping jiminy, she did at that. Grace became Princess Grace when she married Prince Rainier III of Monaco. Imagine the headlines in the newspaper gossip columns: *"Grace Abandons Hollywood!"* That doesn't sound particularly good. Another Grace, the Jefferson

Airplane singer Grace Slick, stayed in California. In the long run, the substances of San Francisco weren't good for Grace. The West coast isn't looking good. Maybe the good graces are on the East coast?

Grace Metalious was from New Hampshire. This Grace wrote the phenomenally successful novel, *Peyten Place*. More than just a best seller in print, it spawned a hit movie *and* a television show. Still, this Grace had similar problems to the last Grace. Outrageous media success doesn't seem to be fertile ground for good graces. Continuing down my list, I don't think we can go wrong with St. Grace. This Grace is the patron saint of Valencia, Spain. Saints are generally a safe bet in the *good* department. Yikes, there's a bit of a weapons problem I didn't expect. In her portraits, St. Grace is usually seen holding an axe. I'm not comfortable enough with axes to commit to a good rating here.

Perhaps good graces aren't people after all. Let's look for good grace things instead. The Chicago Transit Authority had a train station named Grace from 1900 to 1949.[1] Shuttering it after less than fifty years seems a tad suspicious. How can there be an *end of the line* for authentically good grace? If Grace station was really good they would have kept it open.

Next up, the reviews for the "Hamburger Grace" at *Bistro Grace* in Montreal look quite promising. This grace hasn't been shut down like the train station, but it is geographically suspect. Shouldn't good grace, burger or otherwise, be available in more than one location? Of course, there is the chance that geographic grace might be so good that it attracts visitors from all over. Hey, Graceland in Memphis attracts over half a million visitors each year. It's the gated compound that Elvis lived in for years. I have mixed feelings about this land's association with grace. I'm pretty sure good grace isn't surrounded by walls and doesn't need guard dogs. Plus, Graceland charges an admission fee, which doesn't sound much like good grace to me.

For one last shot at good grace geography, let's leave the big cities behind. The Northwest region of the United States looks to be big on grace towns. There are towns named Grace in three adjoining states: Washington, Idaho and Montana. If I have to pick between them, I'm leaning towards Grace, Idaho. This Grace is a town with just shy of one thousand residents. Nonetheless, its school system is big into grace. Their school district includes Grace Elementary School, Grace Junior High School, and Grace High School. This looks like a good grace, but wait … Grace High School is home to the *Grace Grizzlies* Football team! The grizzly bear on their logo is ferocious, and that's not good. Enough with the good grace guesses. We need the real thing.

My grace confusion isn't an unusual situation. Lots of folks have an idea about grace that's akin to Augustine's trouble with time. Remember, Augustine knew what time was until he had to put it into words. The same applies to grace. Let's face it, we're pretty casual about our use of the term. In Christian circles, "grace" is tossed about in a matter-of-fact manner that seems to suggest we have a defined, commonly understood perception of what the term communicates. Without getting all egg-heady, I think that a cursory review of the history of the doctrine of grace quickly dispels this notion. It doesn't take a historian to recognize there's no fixed view of grace, nor even one that is common across all Christian traditions. We may agree that there is a connection between God, grace, and salvation, but discussion beyond that point is a rare commodity in too many church communities. On the noticing front this simply won't do. Grace is big. Grace is important. And, surprise, surprise, grace is *exactly* what we have been exploring since page one of chapter one. No, you haven't been tricked; you have been – and are – graced. Let's take a look at how grace is aligned with the big ideas we've been scouting out. We'll start with a defining headline worth noticing:

GRACE IS GOD'S SELF-COMMUNICATION TO
HUMANKIND.

Here's the fine print: The constant offer of God is God's self-offer to us, which is given as grace, and which we can notice because of grace. Whenever we are talking about God's revelatory communication, or God's gift of God's self to us, we're talking about grace. The same holds true when we talk about our God-given orientation to God; our spirit which seeks fulfillment. Our pre-apprehension *reaching beyond*, which is always a means of referencing our relation to God, is also grace. In other words, there are two key conjoined aspects of grace: God gives the gift of God's self as the offer of human fulfilment, and humankind is graced with the capacity to be aware of God's offer. Think of grace as the message which communicates God's fulfillment invitation, *and* the magnetic pole that orients us to God's invitation. When we talk about pointers, we need to be able to grasp their role in alerting us to grace. When we talk about noticing, we need to grasp that grace encompasses the medium and the message we are noticing. That's why the term "grace" implies communication. Grace is a theological description that takes in the gift and the reception of God's self-offer.

Sometimes language about "God's self" is a little clunky. We use terms like *myself, yourself, herself,* and *himself,* to designate ownership of an action, a posture, an attitude, or an attribute. At the same time, we are usually specifying something more personal than material possession. "Self" language addresses our need to identify things that are indivisibly connected to our *being*. For instance, I can say that I am, myself, the foolish author of my own folly. Here, "*myself*" tells you that my *being* possesses a foolish quality. It seems I have the capacity to make myself foolish; I'm a foolish being. It's like what Popeye, that ever eloquent sailor, said: "I am what I am, and that's all that I am."[2] I can only be that which accurately represents my being.[3] If I give myself in love to another, they get the real me – the only me I have to give. The designation "God's self" is, in the same manner, uniquely about God's *being*. Grace isn't some *thing* that God gives, like a fruit basket or a subscription to *Johnny Notice-Quest* comic books. No, God's grace is God communicating God, as God really is. In Popeye-speak that means God is as God is and is always as God is. God's continuous offer, the one that we all have the freedom to accept or reject, *is* God offering God. And even though God continually addresses us with this divine self-offer, God is never depleted. Grace is continually present and is never diminished.

There are many ways that the title of this book could have tied *noticing* and *grace* together. It could have been called *Noticing Grace*, or *Noticing the Universal Grace of God*, or *Anne of Grace Gables Notices*, or maybe *Holy Pointers and the Chamber of Not-Secret Grace* (yes, even my publisher would reject the last two). The key thing is that whenever we use the words *noticing*, *pre-apprehension*, or *revelation*, we're in the neighbourhood of grace. We notice God's offer because we are graced with the desire to seek, and the capacity to notice. Presence, which has been a huge recurring theme for us, is also intimately aligned with grace. God's presence reveals God's self-offer, and wherever God's self-offer is addressed, grace is present.

As long as we're connecting dots, the connection between presence and participation mustn't escape our notice. Our focus has been on *our* interaction and engagement. There is also the Three-is-One participation that's unique to the Holy Trinity to consider. The apostle Paul's second letter to the church in Corinth draws our attention to this beautifully. I'm not telling tales when I say that Paul's letters could be chatty.

Nor am I off-base saying that he understood the value of a memorable greeting and farewell blessings. Paul used these pleasantries in his letters to say hello, to spread the love, and to focus his readers on harmonious living "*in Christ.*" Paul repeatedly declared that believers are "in Christ" to highlight that Christians are united with Jesus (the Christ or *anointed one,* of God). The Church as a body participates *in Christ* as we participate with one another (Romans 12:3-5). We're going to dig further into this down the line. Here and now, I'm pointing to Paul's letter to Corinth because there he spells out the participating presence of grace in longform: "The grace of the Lord Jesus Christ, the love of God, and the communion of the Holy Spirit be with all of you" (2 Corinthians 13:13). The grace offered to us "in Christ" is the communication, participation, guidance, and presence in love of the Holy Trinity. God's grace is the presence of God's revealing self-offer, and simultaneously, a divine invitation to participate.

We live in a world that gives us plenty of opportunities to question claims of God's constancy. How can God's presence be continuous? With all the awful things that go on, there must be gaps where grace is not present. This conclusion presupposes that God's grace isn't present when awful things happen. If this is on your mind, it will likely help if you hear the word *grace* as *self-offer.* Is God's self-offer still on offer when awful things happen? My answer is yes. I've heard numerous personal stories, as a friend and as a pastor, that echo this. Many people find that God's self-offer is most noticeable to them in their darkest hour. The continuous presence of God's self-offer is precisely why the worn-out adage, *there but for the grace of God,* is so misleading and ridiculous. God's continuous presence is a universal self-offer to humankind. It is an offer that doesn't skip anybody, although as we have seen, anybody and everybody has the freedom to reject God's offer. No doubt, some misunderstandings around God's constancy stem from the misguided view that human freedom is a mundane capacity. Think again; freedom is one-hundred proof potent. Having freedom isn't about the right to choose from a smorgasbord of never-ending individual choices. It is far more precious than that. Freedom is the gift to define ourselves in relation to God. We are graced with the capacity to notice God's continuous self-offer. Freedom is the corresponding capacity to accept God's offer.

Does it feel like we're juggling a lot of aspects of grace at the same time? Are there just too many scoops to fit on a single grace cone? Is it muttering time again? Okay, you mutter and I'll listen: "Can't you see that it takes a lot of focus to juggle presence and constancy and revelation and then, *whoops* … I've dropped participation! Too many grace-things, slow down already."

I hear you. When it comes to noticing grace, it can seem like there are a lot of moving parts. If that's the case, just remember to hear the word *grace* as *self-offer*; then your juggling worries are over. God's self-offer has *no* moving parts; the offer is simply God. All of the other aspects that reside in the neighbourhood of grace (presence, constancy, divine participation, etc.), point us to divine mystery. Fellow notices-questers, we spent enough time launching the Noticing Utility Vehicle back in chapter five to know about mystery. That is, we know that we don't *know* divine mystery – we explore and engage divine mystery. Grace, and the *why* questions it prompts, are mystery. *Why* did God choose to reveal the divine self-offer? *Why* did God choose to give us the capacity to notice? *Why* me, *why* you, *why* us? If we go looking for a reason why humankind in some way deserves grace … well, there lies the way of madness. No one has any claim on God's grace. It is never a gift we earn or deserve, or to use the language many theologians lean on: grace is unmerited, it is always received as a gratuitous gift. If you ever feel the need to ask whether God loves us, the answer is the grace of God's continual self-offer to us. In other words, the answer is Yes beyond measure. Grace is loving generosity that invites your participation. Wow.

Having acknowledged that grace has a mysterious side, let's take another line of approach. Our theological toolbelt has a negative side that helps when our positive analogies and comparisons feel exhausted. I don't mean *negative* as in nasty, I mean negation and absence: we'll consider what grace is *not*. I can think of many times that negation has helped me sort things, and many other times I've wished others would notice how it works. For example, there is a long history of actors mistakenly assuming they are singers. Sylvester Stallone acted opposite Dolly Parton in the musical comedy *Rhinestone.* The film tanked but Dolly ably escaped with two top-ten country hits. Stallone, on the other hand, ably demonstrated that he is *not* a singer. Likewise, Clint Eastwood staked his singing claim in the film adaptation of the musical goldmine *Paint Your Wagon.* Unfortunately, he was saddled with singing a little ditty called *I Talk to the Trees.* The much-abused trees, and just about everyone else, would greatly prefer that Eastwood only talk – he is *not* a singer. More recently ex-007 actor Pierce Brosnan sang in the ABBA-fest film adaption of the musical *Momma Mia!* I will say no more than he out-Stalloned Sylvester and out-Eastwooded Clint. Negation to the rescue: I can safely assume these guys are screen actors because I know they are not screen singers.

Negation can also help us avoid cuts and bruises. I know I am not a lumberjack, so I can comfortably propose that I not use chainsaws. Not everyone harnesses the power of effective negation. In 1974, motorcycle stuntman Evel Knievel proposed a jump across the Snake River Canyon in Idaho. The gap was deemed too wide for a standard motorcycle, so he had a steam-powered rocket-cycle built for the occasion. During the jump attempt, Knievel's cleverly named *Skycycle X-2* succumbed to gravity and fell into the canyon. During his parachute free-fall (while still in the cycle capsule), it became evident that a motorcycle is not a rocket, and a motorcycle stuntman is not an astronaut.

So much for song and dance and gravity lessons; what can negation suggest about grace? What two things might get confused when we talk about the presence of grace? Each reader in our group might have a unique slant on this question. As for me, I am fascinated by the relationship grace has with human experience. If we lay this all out, I think it will become apparent that grace and experience are easily confused. Human experience is a constant presence in our lives. We can't escape our *being*, and our *being* is always experiencing something. We can't escape experience by turning it off, or running from it, or by sleeping. Even at our coach-potato laziest we're experiencing the sensation of our respiratory systems. As long as we're breathing, we are experiencing. Even when we're unconscious, our subconscious is plenty conscious. Now, pair that with what we know about grace. God's self-offer is constant, and our graced capacity to seek God is ongoing. That means that grace accompanies all human experience. There is no experience that is separate from the presence of grace. Confused yet? Toto, I've a feeling we're not in Grace, Idaho anymore!

Let's take this exploration to the next level. If grace accompanies our everyday experience, is grace a component of experience? Is experience a component of grace? The core of these questions can be boiled down to a single query: Can we experience grace? We know what it's like to experience weather, and companionship, and birthday cake, because they are not constant. We have all experienced an absence of wind, and friends, and (tragically) cake. None of us can say the same about grace. We haven't experienced the absence of grace any more than we've experienced the absence of *being*. This is quite a knotty situation, because if we haven't experienced the absence of grace, how can we recognize the *presence* of grace? Negation, can you help make heads or tails of this experience of grace dilemma?

Sure. Experience has a sensory foundation. In tandem, our senses physically experience our world and our minds cognitively experience our *being*. Grace is *not* physical. Grace is *not* cognitive. Grace is *not* experience. Using negation, we arrive at the reasonable assumption that grace is not a component of experience, and experience, correspondingly, is not a component of grace. This helps us to not confuse grace for experience. While you ponder this point, I'll express our thanks and say goodbye to negation. Questers, this is where we come up for air only to discover we're facing mystery and knee-deep in nuance. Because as surely as grace is not experience, we experience grace … just not as grace.[4]

As cryptic as experiencing grace *not as grace* sounds, we have mused about a similar idea. Recall how we encounter the presence of God in silence. It isn't the senses or the mind that recognize the presence of God in silence. God's presence is recognized by our spirit. We are spiritual beings whose spirit is oriented to seek God – to reach out for the fulfilment of our humanity in God. The technical term for this is human transcendence. For our graced human spirit to reach out to God, it must transcend the limitations of our bodily senses. Our spirit recognizes God in silence, not as God, but as the spiritual presence of God. In the same manner we experience the grace of God, not as grace, but as spiritual transcendence (or movement) towards God's presence. Spirit movement may be experienced by an individual, or in concert with multiple people. For example, you may be a single participant among a shared sacramental engagement (like a worship service or the celebration of communion). Mystery remains front and center when we seek God. There is no seeking recipe and no transcendence formula. There are no dramatic expectations, but of course, there is always anticipation.

If we plotted our noticing path on a roadmap, it would look like a two-lane thoroughfare. The lanes would appear side-by-side and oriented in the same direction. Both lanes are a single road with a single name: anticipation. Like all two-lane roads, they have the same terminus point – the same end. This roadmap is easily imagined because it mirrors the reality of everyone who seeks God. For all of us, there are two dimensions to our anticipation of God's presence. One dimension takes in our everyday interactions with things, thoughts, and events. This is our life among the pointers through which we notice God's presence in the world. In this here-and-now dimension, our openness to God's self-offer can also perceive the invitation to participate in God's grace in the world.

Running alongside the here-and-now, we have an eternal anticipation. Because zero people have lived forever, we grasp that our chances of living untold eons on Earth are precisely the same: zero. So, if immortality is not in the cards, just what are we anticipating? There are a lot of different terms used by the various corners of Christianity to answer this eternal question. The term that feels most at home for me in all of these varied Christian responses is *fulfillment.* Eternal anticipation is the anticipation of fulfilled humanity and fulfilled harmony. In other words, an anticipation of the fullness of grace. This is the fullness of God's self-disclosure, and the fullness of our acceptance of God's self-offer. As grand as we may imagine the fulfillment of our humanity to be, it is still humanity. The mystery and majesty of God's revelation far exceeds human comprehension. My own anticipation, for that is all any of us can imagine, is that graced fulfillment amplifies (rather than diminishes) the distinction between humankind and God.

Our two-lane anticipation of graced-fulfillment is sometimes described as *now-and-not-yet.* The grace we notice now fills us with wonder, yet we also understand that it is not the fullness of wonder to come. The transcendence that our spirit experiences now in our orientation to God, hints at the full transcendence that is God's fulfillment of our humanity. As with all real mystery, our words fail to do justice to a graced-fulfillment which our anticipation can only faintly imagine. The apostle Paul, who was about as enlightened as we humans get, did find some really good words to describe our anticipation situation:

> Now we see in a mirror, dimly, but then we will see face to face. Now I know only in part; then I will know fully, even as I have been fully known. (1 Corinthians 13:12)

When Paul was around, his ministry kept him busy. He did, however, find time to earn some pocket change as a tent maker. If he was around today, I suspect Paul would do some sideline work as a crossword puzzle editor. In addition to being very good with words, he excelled at helping others fill in the blanks. He also gets bonus marks for recognizing the difference between a puzzle and a real mystery.

There is no side-stepping the obvious mystery of grace, or the limitations of our "dimly" present view. Equally, there's no mistaking the noticeably relational reality of grace. First off, grace is an offer, a self-offer. That means it is addressed to us like a love letter. Also, any offer of self invites engagement and participation. All the pointers in the universe point to this. Every reference to God references this. We are graced with the capacity to notice and receive God's grace, so that we might accept the invitation to participate. This framework to engage our noticing skills and participation can be posed in a simple way: Everything points to God. It can also be posed in Rahner's way, with a little more finesse:

> God's grace (and Christ's) is ... present in everything as the mysterious essence of the whole of reflective reality,

with the result that it is not easy to strive after something without being concerned in one way or another with God (and Christ).[5]

We have *all* been engaged by God's grace. God's self-offer is to *all* humankind, so we have *all* been addressed. The universal nature of grace is at the root of our ability to share our noticing experiences. What differentiates one person's participation from another's is quite familiar to us by now. We have called it "noticing that we've noticed," and have described its out-growth as "conscious engagement." Essentially, this pairs together the awareness of God's offer, with an awareness that a response is required. This is when we discover, perhaps to our great surprise, that we are among the *all* who have been addressed. When we recognize that God's offer is face-to-face with our need to respond, it all becomes very personal. The contemporary theologian Ingolf Dalferth describes this per-sonal scene like this:

> We become aware of God's presence by apprehending ourselves to live in God's presence. We cannot do this without realizing that we have been apprehending God's presence long before we became aware of it. Since this can be true of us only if it is true of everybody, the point of communicating our sense of the presence of God to others is not primarily to tell them about us, but to make them aware of their own life in the presence of God. We represent to them what we apprehend in order to make them aware of what they themselves apprehend.[6]

There is an element of our conscious participation that is broader than a unidirectional response *to* God. Our engage-ment in participation also touches other folks among the *all* of humankind. Less formally, let's call them friends, and family, and neighbours, and acquaintances, and strangers. Does that cover everybody? Good, because grace is generous. It is poured out over everyone and we, as participants, are capable of letting grace spill out of us.

Media correspondents take note: This spillage bit sounds like a great news story. Wouldn't it be a nice change of pace to hear a news report about a significant grace leak on our coasts? A spillage of the grace that overflows and simply *must* go somewhere. There would be no need to bring in heavy equipment to contain the spread. The news report could even have photos from a sandy beach that show the effects of a grace spill on marine and wildlife. In my mind this is a picture of happy otters teaching seals a new dance move. I'm a big fan of otters. Rain or shine, they always look like they're having wiggly fun. It just makes sense to me that exposure to a grace spill would prompt them to share with their neighbours. While this is kind of funny, this fake news isn't so far fetched – I mean the grace spillage part. I prefer not to go on public record regarding the likelihood of otters moonlighting as dance instructors. However, I'll gladly point out that God's constant self-offer to humankind is both received (poured out on us like an intentional spill) and shared. If we take the constant offer of God seriously, we spread the love. We become *agents of grace*.

Would you have volunteered to join our trek if you knew we would encounter a society of "agents"? After years of espionage and secret society thriller bombardment, you have good grounds to be suspicious. Have no fear, agents of grace aren't MI5, CSIS, CIA, or KGB type secret forces. You know, the groups they sometimes call "intelligence" agencies and no one can quite figure out why. Agents of grace are something different altogether. Think about the Supermarionation Thunderbirds and forget those wickedly creepy Jason Bourne Treadstone nuts. For readers who missed this British gem, the Thunderbirds were the 1960's marionette television answer to the James Bond spy craze. Picture a family that lives on a secret

The effects of a grace spill
on marine and wildlife

island, which they use as a base for high-tech rescues (and all-around emergency response good deeds). That's what the Thunderbirds marionettes were secretly doing, even though they appeared to be a normal family. Well, as normal as any family that wears matching uniforms and lives on a secret secluded island. The key thing is that the Thunderbirds mixed with the general populous whenever a mission called for it. Agents of grace are like that, only one better. They don't wait for emergencies to leave seclusion and mix with other folks.

Now that we have the background out of the way, I'll spill the best part. Agents of grace aren't an exclusive society; this group is universally inclusive. That means, you guessed it … you're an agent of grace. All who have received grace have a common mission to be conduits of grace. Participating in the constant offer of God is as simple as sharing the grace you have noticed (in your graced-existence). Agents of grace take a hint from the New Testament letter known as First Peter; a communication addressed to the emerging church in first-century Asia Minor. The author told his readers: "Like good stewards of the manifold grace of God, serve one another with whatever gift each of you has received" (1 Peter 4:10). We are shaped by the grace we have received. Our *being* is graced-being, and our agency and mission is to grace others – to *do grace.* I know, I know, I know … responsible authors shouldn't go around willy-nilly changing nouns into verbs. In my defense I can only say: If we're going to really understand our mission, we have to understand and embrace grace as a verb.

During our negation exercise with Sylvester Stallone, Clint Eastwood, and Pierce Brosnan, we learned what they are by discerning what they are not. Sometimes though, we know things for what they are, and then later for what they become. This is the case when nouns get moulded into verbs. Think back a decade or so to when people would *search* using the Google search engine. Over time a search inquiry became an inquiry we would *google* – the proper noun also became a verb. If you don't believe me, *google* it. When you're done, print out the answer and *xerox* an extra copy. Be a pal and *Fed-Ex* the copy to me overnight, because I'm anxious to get this whole noun-becomes-verb issue settled. In closing, I assert that the Pinocchio story is false, because puppets can't become real boys. Yet, the verb grace is true, because nouns can become real verbs. The prosecution rests its case. If you think you can *beef* up your defence, I'll *book* time to listen.

On our journey, we all have the opportunity to notice God's grace. There are pointers-a-plenty to highlight God's presence in our lives. Having noticed that we noticed, we have the opportunity to choose how we participate in grace. How will we be "good stewards of the manifold grace of God?" How will we radiate the grace of God to illuminate the hope of the world?

8

Hope
(in God, Neighbour, and Ink)

Have you ever tasted Play-Doh? If you were raised in North America, that's a bit like asking whether you have ever been a child. Sneaking a taste of colourful Play-Doh modeling compound has been a rite of passage since the latter 1950's. As far as childhood hazards go, Play-Doh sampling ranks near the bottom end of the danger scale. That's because Doh could pass for dough's quirky second-cousin. It is primarily a mixture of water, salt and flour. It doesn't even pose a risk to kids with peanut or dairy allergies. There is some wheat, so give it a pass if you avoid gluten (or, indeed, if you have any sense at all). The salty modelling compound was first marketed as a wallpaper cleaner. It relocated from home décor to toy shelves for the benefit of all involved (which likely includes you). While there is no accounting for the taste of popular taste, Play-Doh is indisputably popular. The manufacturers of Play-Doh estimate that more than 700 million pounds of the stuff has been produced.[1] It has even been inducted into the National Toy Hall of Fame.[2]

As lovely as our memories of Play-Doh are, we all know there is a dark side to the Doh. It starts out bright and easy to manipulate. Over time it becomes dry and harder to mould. Eventually it settles into what all Play-Doh becomes: a dirt-spotted crumbly lump we can no longer manipulate. There is a day when all Play-Doh players discover they are no longer master of all that they mould. In the end, the arc of our relationship with Play-Doh is a lot like the arc of our relationship to hope.

As children we hope for toys like Play-Doh – amusements with little substance or enduring worth. When the burdens of adolescent self-consciousness encroach on our lives, we hope for *more*. We hope for different fleeting wonders, like a smile from the girl or boy we fancy in high school. By the time we enter adulthood our eyes are a little wider open. Adulthood remoulds our relationship to hope. With the ups and downs of life, the victories and bruises we accumulate progressively reshape us and reshape our hopes. An amusement or a smile give momentary solace, but our towering big-ticket hopes are companionship, comfort, health, constancy, and security. Increasingly we can see the trajectory of our lives unfolding before us. The material and fleeting hopes of youth get coated in adult grit. Eventually hope becomes fixed into a form we can no longer attempt to manipulate. This is where hope becomes real; where hope becomes a matter of faith. Hope becomes faith in the presence, promises, and perseverance of God's constancy, or it becomes despair.

Mature adult hope is never neutral or dispassionate. Hope follows the heart. Noticing the constancy and presence of grace leads us to notice that the hope of our heart – the hope of our *being* – is real. When we surrender to despair, which we all do at times, our hope runs the risk of hardening and crumbling like ancient Play-Doh. As odd as it may seem, a taste of Play-Doh experience can help us think about our relationship with hope. Recalling our Play-Doh days reminds us how severely the taste stakes change in adulthood. The taste of childhood Play-Doh may be naively salty, but the taste of adult despair is hardened bitterness. Noticing is a potent antidote to bitterness. When we consciously participate in God's self-offer, we broadcast our hope so others might see, notice, and embrace hope.

Admittedly, we're unlikely to engage others in a conversation about Play-Doh as an *entrée* to discussing hope. Hope is a serious business, and frankly, Play-Doh isn't. Christian hope is usually something we align with our anticipation of fulfillment in God. At our core, we hold to the hope that is promised for humankind in the death and resurrection of Jesus. For all of our diverse attempts to articulate the nuts and bolts of our resurrection hope, we inevitably must bow to the mystery of grace. The resurrection of Jesus, the fullest self-revelation of God among us, is the revelation of the divine mastery over death that mediates human restoration to God. In anticipation terms, the resurrection has initiated the overlapping eras of *now* and *not yet*. That means that the resurrection is the basis for our *now* hope, and our anticipation of humanity's fulfillment hope. Trying to speak about the scope of hope is a lot like trying to articulate the magnitude of grace. Hope is another way that we are invited to participate in the panorama of God's mystery.

Whenever our journey path has veered into mystery territory, there has been a risk that some of us will begin to feel disconnected. There are times when facing mystery feels like reaching out for a vapour we cannot grasp. How, on earth, can we hold on to mystery? Ditto for the intangibles that surround hope. Mystery, you may recollect, is not synonymous with distance. It is also intimately close. A little noticing might help illuminate just how connected our graced-orientation to God is to our concrete lives. In this vein, Karl Rahner made a point of reminding us of the connection between hope, faith, and mystery: "If hope is not to belie its own essence, it can tolerate no definitive limits. But where it exists and sustains the whole person, takes the whole person out of herself and into this mystery we call God, it can and must also believe in Jesus' resurrection."[3] This personal embrace of the mystery of the resurrection is a trait Rahner called, "the courage of hope."[4] Hope is a companion we connect with and embrace as close as any other in our lives. There is a bleakness that inevitably comes when the embrace of hope is broken. Commenting on this reality, Rahner stated that, "Apart from hope there is only despair. We can certainly dismiss despair and suppress it, but without hope it is sure to return, and without freely accepted hope it does return."[5] We feel disconnected when we allow distance to impede our embrace of hope. In such times take heart, hope is like a compassionate loved one to whom we can always return.

There is nothing novel about despair; it has been a continuous plague on humanity. There is a breed of poets who romanticize and wallow in it, but in truth, despair is in all ways awful. In the Psalms we find ancient testimonies to the fragility of human existence, and the strength that faith distills from hope. Despair, faith, and hope are laid out for all of us in this excerpt from Psalm Thirty-Nine:

I was silent and still;
    I held my peace to no avail;
my distress grew worse,
    my heart became hot within me.
While I mused, the fire burned;
    then I spoke with my tongue:

"Lord, let me know my end,
    and what is the measure of my days;
    let me know how fleeting my life is.
You have made my days a few handbreadths,
    and my lifetime is as nothing in your sight.
Surely everyone stands as a mere breath.
    Surely everyone goes about like a shadow.
Surely for nothing they are in turmoil;
    they heap up, and do not know who will gather.

And now, O Lord, what do I wait for?
My hope is in you." (Psalm 39:2-7)

The anguish of the psalmist is real, but so is his hope. How is it that hope can remain strong among all the weighty concerns that prey on our human weaknesses? I suspect that Augustine was pondering this after he was asked to write a portable handbook on the pillars of the Christian life. In response he came up with a treatise on faith, hope, and love, in which he asks, "Is it possible to hope for what we do not believe in?"[6] This gets to the heart of why the psalmist in the shackles of despair can declare, "My hope is in you." It is simply *not* conceivable to hope for what we do not believe in. It is conceivable and evident that the psalmist's hope is preserved in faith. It is his faith that we notice because it illuminates hope in a sea of darkness and despair. It is hope worth noticing precisely because it points to God. As extraordinary as it may seem, the hope that illuminates us points others to the constant offer of God.

We are material pointers with spiritual potency. There's a rather cool thing that goes along with this: as you and I participate in grace, other people are pointers that not only reference God – they also reference us (as we reference God)! This might sound a wee bit tricky, but it's a vehicle for hope that has been handed down for eons. You might know it as *the love of God and the love of neighbour*. This is a shorthand way to reference some of the most significant and practical teachings in scripture. In the *Gospel According to Mark*, there is an account of Jesus affirming that the primary commandments are to "love the Lord your God with all your heart, and with all your soul, and with all your mind, and with all your strength," and to "love your neighbor as yourself" (Mark 12:30-31).[7] Note that Jesus wasn't teaching anything radical or novel. He was *affirming* commandments that had been established in ancient

Israel. Love of God and love of neighbour are principles that were already known by every man, woman and child Jesus taught (Deuteronomy 6:5; Leviticus 19:18).

In the twenty-first century we don't deal well with words like "commandment." This can be confirmed with a simple experiment: take a friend out for burgers, and then *command* that they fetch some ketchup from the proprietor. You can probably imagine how well that would go down. If not, be prepared for some abuse (that may include an airborne tomato product). It's alright, we don't need to push back at *commandment*. Instead, think of *love of God and love of neighbour* like you would a family motto. Except, it's a motto that extends to all families. I must confess that it is substantially better than the family motto I passed on to my sons: *Don't buy "fresh" seafood from the back of a truck with Iowa plates.* Yes, knowing not to procure roadside lobster in land-locked states is a marker of true wisdom, but it's not really a principle to live your entire life by.

The apostle Paul didn't formally identify a motto, but if he needed to, *love God and love your neighbour* would qualify as a serious contender. In Paul's letter to the Christian community in Rome he cites a passel of commandments, then sums them up with a single phrase: "Love your neighbor as yourself" (Romans 13:9). When he commented on Paul's message, Rahner took a step back to point out how Paul's words fit in the big picture. Rahner wrote: "If we speak of God, or love, or the mystery of human life, or eternity, we are speaking of one and the same thing, in which everything is summed up as in its head."[8] Everything points to God, and nothing points more emphatically than our love for God, as it loves our neighbour. That is how our illuminating hope in God illuminates hope in our neighbour. This is how the faith that embraces hope is recognized in us. It's no wonder that Augustine wrote a portable handbook on faith, hope, and love. They are exactly what we want to have close at hand whenever we encounter our neighbour. So, Augustine, "Is it possible to hope for what we do not believe in?"[9] No. Hope follows the faith of our heart, and both are sustained by the love of God.

Way back in chapter three we wrestled with a predicament I'll politely call "the *NSYNC problem." You'll recall the question we faced with this star-studded conundrum: How do we handle boy band reunion splinter groups? The answer was – and will be again when Harry Styles and the *One Direction* boys need a cash infusion – mediation. In the end, our important *NSYNC lesson had, unsurprisingly, absolutely nothing to do with boy bands. The key takeaway was that Jesus of Nazareth is uniquely the only person in history to be both a meditator between humankind and God, *and* the unmediated presence of God on earth. Rahner had this truth in mind when he wrote about our participation in the love of God, mediated by Christ. He used the term *intercommunication* to describe the mediation of God's self-communication in our interactions with others.

In essence, to participate in "human intercommunication" is to love one's neighbour by participating in the grace that defines our relationship with God. When we love our neighbour, we are in concert with Christ's mediation of God's self-offer. Each act of love exists as a single event within the universal event of God's self-revealing grace. In this way we participate in communicating God's invitation to salvation – God's invitation to graced-fulfillment. The role of Jesus as God's incarnate mediating presence is absolutely key here. As Rahner put it, in the incarnation "God himself has become our neighbour. In every neighbour, then, this one neighbour, who is most near and most far is accepted and loved."[10]

Another way to approach our participation is to recognize it as sharing love, in response to receiving God's gift of love. The very love that we have to share is derived from and sustained by God's love. The love in which grace is freely given, is the same love we respond to God with, and give to others. Our love is always us participating in, and sharing, the grace that is continuously present to us. Our role in inter-communication mustn't be thought of as *us* making love of neighbour happen. We're in the participation bus, but we're most definitely not driving. Grace isn't ever something that we create. Our participation always points to the grace we are striving to notice; the grace which is the basis of our hope.

The muttering is beginning to build. It sounds something like: "Yikes, can he really be serious about me loving *all* my neighbours? I've got some big-time shady neighbours with appallingly noisy guard dogs." All of us could join your chorus because we're all selective with our neighbourly love. I get your concern; we all have a list of reasons to hunker down in a fortress of self-interest. Incidentally, Rahner appreciated how hard it is to add *love neighbour* to our *love God* motto, and he never downplayed the difficulty of loving unconditionally. In fact, Rahner called it "the ultimate reality and the hardest task of our lives."[11] But he also said that:

> If we have turned in love from self to our neighbour, we have come to God, not by our strength but by God's grace. God who, as John says [in 1 John 4], had loved us so that we might love our neighbour, has truly laid hold of us, has torn us as it were from self and given us what in conjunction constitutes eternity, a personal union with others in which we are united to God.[12]

A personal union with others that unites us in the love of God, is the *now* we enjoy while anticipating the *not yet* of God's fulfillment. In other words: if *not yet* is the hope of eternity, then the grace that unites us with others to God is the hope of *now*.

All this interaction with mediation has put me in a mood for reminiscing about bygone chapters. As much as I enjoyed our reprise of the *NSYNC caper, I miss our heady time-travelling exploits even more. It seems like it was only three chapters ago when we dared to ask, what is time? All things considered, there are very good reasons for this. It *was* only three chapters ago, and we did muck about a bit with time. Well, that was then ... what about *now*? - - - - That's not a rhetorical device, I really mean it: what about *now*? In our time-travelling days we explored the relationship of time and eternity. Is there a similar connection between our *now* hope and the future hope we anticipate? As sure as the brook runs to the river, there's a connection. Before we say good-bye to Rahner for a while, we'll let him explain it with a fanciful scenario:

> If someone had already lit the fuse for a tremendous explosion, but was still waiting for the explosion which will follow with dreadful certainty, that person certainly would not say that the lighting of the fuse was an event of the past. The beginning of the event which is still in course of development but is moving inexorably and irresistibly toward its culmination, is not past but is a kind of present, and already contains its future; it is a movement which continues by comprising past and present in a present real unity. These concepts must be clear if we are to attempt to say something meaningful about the Lord's resurrection.[13]

Did you have the resurrection in mind, or have you just had another *déjà vu* are-we-here-again flash? You'll be okay, there's no *déjà voodoo* at work here. Let me reassure you that we aren't going in circles. We haven't *returned* to the Lord's resurrection because throughout our exploration of hope, we have never left it behind. The future hope we are seeking to connect with our present hope is all wrapped up in the past, present, and future reality of the resurrection. The fuse of hope has been lit, is *now* lit, and is moving toward the future it already contains. In other words: the hope promised in the resurrection of Christ is now with us, and already contains the grace which fulfills our destiny. Hope truly is now, truly resides in grace, and truly is ours to participate in. Notice up!

One of the best things about long-distance quests is that there's oodles of time to share stories. One of the great things about being the author who gets to drive, is that no one in the back seat can interrupt with the classic *are we there yet* question. Sure, you can mutter all you like, but I'm in charge of the words and I'm shutting down all *when do we get there* whining. Remember, it's a noticing-quest – we don't ever run out of grace to notice. That's a super important point when you're on a pointer-noticing journey that routinely messes with time, eternity, then, now, and whenever. If it's your turn in the back seat of the Noticing Utility Vehicle, settle down. We're on our way – but don't be foolish – of course we're not there yet. There's lots of time for stories and I've got one up my sleeve. Actually, I've got two up my sleeves: one on each arm.

If it's a sunny summer short-sleeve day, the world can plainly see that my left arm has a word tattooed on it. That lefty word is *grace*. And while I have been accused of being unbalanced at times, my arms never are. That's because I have another word tattooed on my right arm. The right word is *hope*. For those of you skimming through this book at a friend's place, or after exhausting the old magazines in your dentist's office, don't mistake the significance of my inky words. I'm not one of those hardcore Scrabble warriors by any means. For those who have actually read this far, I freely admit that my tattoos are highly representative of my Scrabble prowess. Four and five letter words containing the most common vowels in the English alphabet, really are about my speed. *Hope* is good for ten points, and *grace* garners a mere eleven. Even with a triple word square, neither of these words will crush my Scrabble foes. So, no, these words aren't about Scrabble. My hand-crafted ink stains point (at least in my mind) to the fourth chapter of the *Gospel According to Luke*. In that chapter Luke describes a sabbath day visit by Jesus to his hometown synagogue. In the presence of his hometown crowd, Jesus read aloud the words of the prophet Isaiah:[14]

> The Spirit of the Lord is upon me, because he has anointed me to bring good news to the poor. He has sent me to proclaim release to the captives and recovery of sight to the blind, to let the oppressed go free, to proclaim the year of the Lord's favour. (Luke 4:18-19)

Jesus then introduced a new depth of meaning to these well-known words by announcing: "Today this scripture has been fulfilled in your hearing" (Luke 4:21). There is nothing ambiguous about this statement; Jesus is proclaiming liberation in a multitude of manifestations. Whether we are poor in spirit, are captive to the exploitation and consumption pressures of economic systems, have lost sight of hope, or are oppressed by hostile forces, we have received "good news." Christ's presence in human history is the fullest revelation of God's invitation. This is the apex of grace – nothing is more significant. Christ proclaiming our release from the captivity of despair is the height of hope. This passage from Luke is the most beautiful definition of hope I can imagine. It is the grace of God revealed as an invitation, and a proclamation that hope exists in God's presence *now*.

The words Jesus spoke point to the emancipation of all who accept God's self-offer. The words indelibly etched on my arms are a portable nine-letter summary: grace, hope. They may not

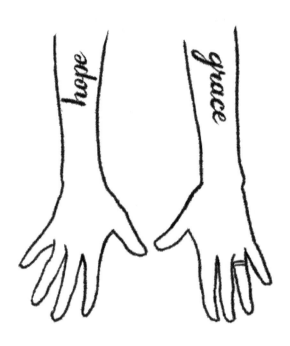

No, these words aren't
about Scrabble

add up to riches on a Scrabble board, but don't let that fool you. The grace of God and the hope it brings is the genuine definition of wealth. Grace is generous and abundant. Hope becomes real when we point to that abundance.

While there is no misreading the promise of hope, I can't say the same for my tattoos. I was walking in a park with my wife a few days after *grace* and *hope* were tattooed on my arms. The ink was so fresh that the words practically jumped off my skin. They caught the attention of a gentleman who was walking towards us on the park path. The man paused in front of us, looked down at my arms and then up at my wife. Giving me a smile, he pointed to my wife and asked, "Is she Grace?" Yes, that was the moment I clued in to the obvious fact that grace and hope are also women's names. Apparently one man's pointers to liberation are another man's tribute to some girls named Grace and Hope. I would like to report that I made the most of this intercommunication opportunity. Alas, I was too dumbfounded to kick my tongue into language mode. Lost for words, I offered a smile to the grace-spotter and continued on. From time to time I wonder whether he recognized my forearms as pointers to the source of grace and hope, and was just messing with me. Heaven forbid. Messing with grace has been known to have serious side effects.

Most of the ways we find to share God's love with our neighbours are the run-of-the-mill everyday variety. Some-times though, we are drawn to encounters that we plan for. I would offer one of my own stories to describe this, but my favourite planned encounter story isn't actually mine, it belongs to Jimmy Carter. Yes, I'm not pulling a fast one on the listeners in the back seat. This story has been told by *the* Jimmy Carter; the one who leveraged his past-president profile to launch the Carter Center. This nonprofit and nongovern-mental organization works to resolve conflicts, uphold human rights, and improve health care. There are many reasons to take note of the choices Carter has made, but two particularly resonate with me. The first is that President Carter is the only Western leader I am aware of who made time to teach Sunday School while in office. That's right, on fourteen occasions he led classes at First Baptist Church in Washington while he was president. How much free time do you think the American president has to play with? Just about zero? Yeah, that's the same answer I came up with. I guess that means that Carter thinks participating in his faith community is quite important. The second reason is related to the first. It has to do with a story Carter shared in one of his Sunday School classes.

In the period between serving as a state senator and as governor of Georgia, Carter participated in a week-long missionary initiative in Springfield, Massachusetts. His days in Springfield were spent visiting and witnessing to Spanish speaking families. Many of these families had come to the area from Puerto Rico. Recalling his visit, Carter states that his Spanish was fine for reading Scripture, but unsteady when it came to casual conversation. Fortunately, he was partnered with a Cuban-American pastor from Brooklyn named Eloy Cruz. Carter was amazed at Cruz's profound ability to open up and connect with strangers. Cruz's humility and gentle nature so impressed Carter that, before parting, he asked Cruz what made him so effective as a Christian witness. The answer he received stuck with Carter, and upon hearing it, has stuck with me for years. Cruz simply responded that he always tried to follow a simple rule. We've all heard this rule before – so many times that some ears likely hear it as a cliché. However, the words Cruz chose shook all the dust away from this oft-heard phrase, casting fresh light on ancient wisdom. He said: "You only have to have two loves in your life: for God, and for the person in front of you at any particular time."[15] With these words Cruz gives us an astonishing insight into what love of God and love of neighbour *really* means. At any – and all –

particular times, God and neighbour are our two loves. I find this incredibly helpful when I'm forgetting what my neighbour looks like. My neighbour is the person in front of me who I love in conjunction with God.

More than a decade after first hearing Carter's story, the punch line still sends shockwaves through my life. Looking at a person and recognizing that *they are* "the person in front of you at any particular time" can be overwhelming, and even intimidating. Why is this? Is it because our neighbour now has a face? No, our neighbours have always had faces. I think it is powerful because the neighbour we are to love now has a defined and undisputable *place* in our lives. Our neighbour is, inescapably and at all times, whoever we encounter. Acknowledging this, we must reimagine what the hope of God looks like for our neighbour. The hope of God's love looks like us.

Throughout our notice-quest it's been inevitable that each of us must eventually confront the toughest pointer question of all: to whom do I point? I am, by my very being, a reference to God. If I don't notice that crucial truth in myself, how effectively will it be noticed by others? This isn't a matter of pumping up the grace volume by visiting strangers in Springfield, Massachusetts, Missouri, Manitoba, Oregon, Ohio, or Ontario (or wherever the Simpsons live). Planned encounters are a fine way to involve some, but it's our everyday garden variety neighbour interaction that involves everyone. We don't need to block time for this on our calendars because we're already in the thick of things. This means we need to resist recasting love of God and love of neighbour into the contemporary notion of *making myself available*. Does this idea presuppose that there are times when we are *not* available to love God and neighbour? Please, let's give "making myself available" a gold watch and a day-old retirement cake. When we're doing our self-noticing, let's remember not to belittle the importance of everyday interaction. If we spend too much time gawking at the folks scaling the highest peaks, we're going to miss the real action among our neighbours in the base camp. Rahner noted this foothills activity in his description of loving neighbour: "This love is rather the most authentic dimension of life, even though it mostly but not always is done through things a normal person would do in any case."[16] Got it? Once we notice the place that our neighbours have in our lives, we notice opportunities to point to hope for what they are: constant.

One of the niftier facts unearthed in our exploration of grace was that folks like to live in towns called Grace. After sifting through the options, we identified Grace, Idaho as a particularly promising grace-burg. No doubt you are intrigued and have been looking for an excuse to visit Idaho. Let me give you one (I've got plenty of excuses to spare). I'll spell it out: When you go, and inevitably find yourself attending a football game at Grace High School (go Grizzlies!), you'll be well placed to connect Grace to Hope. Simply go to the top row of the bleachers and point in the direction of Fairbanks, Alaska. Remember to bring a powerful telescope with you; one that can see across 1450 kilometres (that's 900 miles in Idahoan). When you look in the direction of Fairbanks, you'll be able to see the town of Hope, British Columbia. Hope is known to many for its portrayal of the fictional Liggett County in Sylvester Stallone's *Rambo: First Blood* movie.[17] That's right, they pass it off as Washington state, but it's actually Hope.

I confess that I have never seen a Rambo film, but I have seen the "District of Hope - Good Neighbour Bylaw No. 1240," which was enacted in 2008.[18] This document is an example of the municipal power of "Don't." "Don't" is one of the things that town councils are elected to tell people. For example, the aforementioned Hope bylaw states that I will be fined if I cruise through town with a mobile public address system and loudly broadcast "Liggett County is a hoax," without first obtaining a permit. And don't even think of spray painting this bogus county warning "on any wall, fence, building or structure that is located on real property and adjacent to a highway or other public place." That would contravene subsection 6.7.

Fellow questers, don't get me wrong. We've been journeying together for many chapters, and I don't for one minute think any of you have latent bylaw-contravening tendencies. We're simply getting the bylaw don'ts of Hope out of the way so that, in contrast, we'll recognize the real *do* of real hope. No letter writer has captured the real do of hope better than the apostle Paul. In his letter to the church in Colossi, Paul said, "Whatever you do, in word or deed, do everything in the name of the Lord Jesus" (Colossians 3:17). Rahner, who gives Paul a run for his money in the run-on sentence sweepstakes, revisited Paul's *do* in one of his homilies:

> Paul says: we must do everything in the name of Jesus. In the Bible the name is equivalent to the person. To speak of someone's name is to speak of someone's person; it conjures up the presence of the person. So when something is done in a person's name, it is done by that person's power and by his commission. Thus acting in a person's name is acting by his or her commission. If we are speaking of God, this means acting in the power of his grace, in a frame of mind that is worthy of God, inspired by God; it means acting in vital union with God ....[19]

If our words and deeds are doing the words and deeds of Jesus, we are "acting in vital union with God." Then, when we notice ourselves noticing our selves, we will see our participation in the hope proclaimed by the life and resurrection of Jesus. This is our hope, and the hope of our neighbours. In short: it is hope expressed in love and love expressed in hope. And, as our now familiar friend Rahner said, "if it is true that over our lives there hovers a boundless love which is never exhausted, which gathers everything into the infinite mystery of God, then we can believe and hope and love."[20] Of course when we believe and hope and love, others notice us pointing to the source of belief and hope and love. Yes, love is a many splendored thing. The love of God is so magnificent that it really deserves its own chapter. So, what are you waiting for ... turn the page to love.

9

Love
(in Neon and Whispers)

Let's assume that every extraterrestrial crop circle story you have ever heard is true. That's right, I'm asking you to momentarily embrace the idea that aliens are shredding our wheat fields into complex geometric shapes. You don't have to become a full blown cereologist (the vaguely scientific sounding moniker for crop circle enthusiasts).[1] No, you just have to acknowledge alien crop circles long enough to ask the obvious question: why us? Of all the planets in all of the galaxies, why disrupt *our* breakfast cereal production? Aliens take note: we have the technology to shred our own wheat (thank you very much). I've given this pressing question some thought and think I have a plausible answer. If there are aliens, they aren't really concerned with our nominal interest in shredded wheat. Even from their distant space ship observatories, our preference for corn flakes should be evident. It seems more likely that the aliens are trying to make sense of our primary preoccupation: love. They just want to know why we are so enamoured with love.

If we put ourselves in the aliens' shoes (or whatever they wear), this love theory looks quite sound. Alien space ships monitoring activity on Earth would very quickly identify our love fixation. Love pervades our society. We sing about it, read books about it, watch movies and plays about it, fill our language with ways to describe it, and build entire industries around chasing it. The evidence is incontrovertible. Consider this: Perry Como had the top pop hit of 1946 with the song *Prisoner of Love*. Thirty years later Paul McCartney and Wings propelled *Silly Love Songs* to the top slot in 1976. Forty years later, Justin Bieber topped the 2016 chart with the song *Love Yourself*. If time marches on, clearly our love fixation matches it stride for stride. Incidentally, I suspect that these three songs are the primary reasons why the aliens are sculpting disc-shaped messages in our wheat. If we could accurately decipher the circles, I believe we would discover that they say: "Perry Como was bad enough, but Bieber is the last straw. Stop it … stop it now!" Of course, this is just a theory.

Love, or what we mistake for it, saturates all of our cultural mediums. Harlequin Romance novels have been around since Perry Como's teen idol heyday. Their literary love tales have sold close to *seven billion* books, and have been translated into more than thirty languages.[2] If that isn't enough to confirm how global the love phenomenon is, just watch a few hundred Hallmark romance movies. By the time you've finished watching they will have made a few hundred more. The folks who produce the Hallmark series of formulaic movies have a recipe that can be replicated indefinitely. They simply recast the lead searching-for-love actor and tweak the backdrop setting. This is easy to do because people in all walks of life are looking for love. Don't believe me? Just ask the high-powered executive in Hallmark's *Anything for Love*, the struggling fashion designer in *Love on the Sidelines*, the widowed mom in *Summer Love*, the aspiring chief in *A Dash of Love*, the travel writer in *Love on the Slopes*, the cooking show producer in *Cooking with Love*, the single woman with a newly adopted dog in *Love at First Bark*, the bad boy hockey player in *Frozen in Love*, the army veteran in *Love and Honor*, the dance instructor in *Love at First Dance*, the coffee shop owner in *Brimming with Love*, or even the tabloid reporter in *Love Exclusively*. They'll tell you that they have a longing for love. However, if you still harbour doubts, I recommend that you also talk to some real people: any people from any corner of the world. We may not all see a connection between alien love curiosity and crop-circles, but I think we can agree that we all desire love.

When we look past the pie-eyed happy endings of Hallmark and Harlequin fiction, it becomes apparent that we love-seekers have a mixed record of success. Knowing this, we're not shy about investing time and money into boosting our relationship odds. A survey conducted by the Pew Research Center in Washington found that thirty percent of adults in the United States have used an online dating site or app. Among adults eighteen to twenty-nine years old, a whopping forty-eight percent of their survey respondents used these services.[3] We're actively pursuing love, but are we so busy looking for new love and more love, that we miss noticing constant love?

If genuine love is revealed by the extent that a lover attends to the needs of their beloved, then God is the love benchmark. God's love for us shines through in a mind-boggling arraying of gifts. The really obvious gifts, like panoramic landscapes and glowing sunrises, stand out like mega-watt neon signs. Sunrises and mountaintop views are feasts for our senses and our intellect. They are big and bright, and fuel our human spirit with wide-eyed wonderment. We can't help but notice their iridescent splendor, just as we notice the loving warmth of an embrace. This neon love is wonderful; from newbies on up to black-belt notice-questers, we all notice and bask in this light. These love events are like a gigantic birthday bouquet of roses. We notice them because they pierce the sameness of the untold number of days when we sleep through the sunrise and no flowers arrive. There is more to these neon love events than first meets the eye. They occur intermittently, like street lights that allow us to notice the dimmer stretches between them. The big and bright signs of God's love help stir us to notice the subtle gentle ones. The multitude of days in which we sleep through the sunrise *are* awash in God's love. Like a constant hum murmuring in the background, God's love is always present.

It is a curious thing that every person who has ever said God doesn't love humankind has been breathing while they complain. Breathing is an extraordinarily powerful example of subtle love. We don't typically spend much time marvelling at the gift of breath. Yet, it is the life-sustaining undercurrent of each and every day. To notice this is to notice God's love tending to the needs of God's beloved. Anyone who has struggled to breathe has noticed the gift of each successive breath. In my young parenting days, I lay with my asthmatic child as he laboured to breathe. When the certainty of breathing is in question, the subtlety surrounding breath vanishes. Each breath is noticed for the gift of love that it is.

The constancy of God's love is as far reaching as the constancy of God's presence. Rahner wrote that, "The rare flower of God's love can bloom quietly, somehow alien and lonely, on lofty peaks or in forgotten valleys of this earth, or it can do so magnificently, in full view of society."[4] No place, and no one, is off limits to God's love. It is universally addressed to humankind in God's constant self-offer. God's love is encountered at every turn and is the basis for God's fullest revelation in Jesus. One of the most treasured verses in all of scripture states that "God is love." This was written in the letter known as First John, in response to God's outpouring of love in Jesus. It states that, through the revelation of Jesus, "We have known and believe the love that God has for us. God is love, and those who abide in love abide in God, and God abides in them" (1 John 4:16). Love is never impersonal, and the love that abides "in God" is deeply intimate. In love we are in God, and God is in us. This is why the same passage of scripture declares that "we know that we abide in God and God in us, because he has given us of his Spirit" (1 John 4:13). If we want to discern what it means to say "God is love," we have all that we need in this passage from First John. God's love is not an emotional afterthought to God's plan for the world. It is, rather, God's orientation to God's own creation. God's love orientation is known to us in God's presence, God's revelation in Jesus, and God's in-dwelling gift of the Holy Spirit. This is God's love expressed threefold in the Holy Trinity by which we know God. We need to notice this.

When it came to pointing out the source of love, the author of First John had a distinct advantage over us. You can bet your bottom dollar he had never heard – or heard of – the British invasion. I don't mean the kind of invasion that kept Napoleon up at night. I mean the Liverpudlian lads who spearheaded the mop top invasion of our North American airwaves. We've all heard *She Loves You* (*Yeah Yeah Yeah*) so many times, that we're somewhat desensitized to the magnitude of the word "love."

Let's hit the reset button and learn love anew: God is love, and love has *always* made the world go around. Always? Yes, always! Bear with me a moment and I'll demonstrate that you can count on this, because no one loses with the love of God. If you'll forgive my baseness: taking a chance on the love of God is like being a participant on a favourably rigged game show. Everyone is a winner just by turning up. It's like this: let's say I'm a game show host, and my show is called *Wheel of Love Fortune*. The game *revolves* around a giant spinning wheel, which is labeled with the dates of a couple of hundred different bygone years. If I selected you to spin the *Wheel of Love Fortune*, I guarantee that you would win every time. That's because every year is knee-deep in the love of God. For the skeptical among us, I'm willing to demonstrate this with a whirl of the wheel. Okay, here goes: *click, click, click, click, click, click...c_l_i_c_k*. The wheel landed on the year 1640. Jackpot!

This was a banner year for noticing the love of God. It's the year that Nicholas Herman of Hériménil, a modest village in north-eastern France, took up residence in Paris.[5] Nicholas was, and is, better known by his chosen name, Brother Lawrence of the Resurrection (ca. 1614-1961). Lawrence was a man who noticed the constant love of God. As long as we're taking a trek time-out to take liberties with time and fictitious game shows, let's also pause to notice Lawrence.

The new residence that Lawrence entered in 1640 was a monastery run by the Order of the Discalced Carmelites of the Blessed Virgin Mary of Mount Carmel. This name is more than a mouthful, so the monastic order was more commonly known as the Discalced Carmelites. "Discalced" is taken from a Latin description of their footwear, or lack of footwear. The Carmelite friars, like most poor people of the era, wore sandals or went barefoot. Lawrence was a lay brother, not an educated priest, and had served as a soldier in the Thirty Years War. The events of his war service disturbed him, and a near fatal injury left him with a physical handicap and lifelong chronic pain.

Lawrence's first assignment in the monastery was working in the kitchen. For his first fifteen years in the order, he cooked for a community that grew to over one hundred members. When his injuries, compounded by gout, made the burden of physical kitchen work too difficult, he took on cobbler duties. In the sandal repair shop (of the *barefoot* friars), he could sit while mending the hundred pairs of sandals he maintained. Until he died at the age of seventy-seven, Lawrence's chosen life was a cycle of manual labour, prayer, and arduous monastery errands that exasperated his physical pain. All things considered; you may be wondering how I can hold up 1640 as a banner year for noticing the love of God. Where was the love of God in this poor injured soldier's life of painful manual labour? The answer must come from Lawrence himself; it is not mine to give. Fortunately, Lawrence wrote a series

Spin the *Wheel of Love Fortune*
I guarantee you will win

of spiritual maxims, left behind a trail of letters, and impressed others so much they recorded their conversations with him. These insights have been published under the title *The Practice of the Presence of God.*[6] They tell Lawrence's story directly in his own words, and in the words he shared with others.

When Lawrence was eighteen years old, he was over-whelmed by a sudden eureka-awareness of the presence of God. He described the life-changing event to a young Parisian abbot named Joseph de Beaufort, with whom he held four conversations during 1666 and 1667. Beaufort wrote this record of Lawrence's account:

> One day in winter while Brother Lawrence was looking at a tree stripped of its leaves, and he realized that in a little while its leaves would reappear, followed by its flowers and fruit, he received a profound insight into God's providence that has never been erased from his soul. This insight completely freed him from the world, and gave him such a love for God that he could not say it had increased during the more than forty years that had passed.[7]

A barren tree may not seem like eureka transformation material, but hey, I've heard that said about garbage bins as well. Let's not forget that the "everything" in *everything points to God*, includes all manner of pines and pears and firs and flowers. Even when they're bare of blooms, they have the potential to be prime eureka-inducing botanical pointers. *Genus Pinus* (pine trees) can also be *Deus-Noticus Eurekus* (flora that alters your orientation to God). Lawrence's love for God grew exponentially with his awareness that God actively loves the whole of creation. God's providence is the divine loving care that guides and nurtures us. It is present in the world with God's presence in the world. Lawrence captured this truth in his spiritual maxims when he wrote: "The holiest, most ordinary, and most necessary practice of the spiritual life is that of the presence of God. It is to take delight in and become accustomed to God's divine company."[8] These words are unmistakeably drawn from Lawrence's personal experience.

Lawrence described the practice of the presence of God as the conscious act of remembering God's presence. Such remembrance is prompted by our mind's imagination and understanding. Lawrence variously referred to the discipline as a habitual "general and loving awareness of God," as "silent conversation with God," and simply as "attention to God."[9] This practice was central to Lawrence's everyday existence. In his written reflections, he credits conscious noticing as a practice which strengthens hope, and renders faith "more intense and efficacious in all life's situations, and especially in times of need."[10] The delight Lawrence experienced while practicing the presence of God is all the more remarkable when we consider that his hands were generally busy with repetitive menial tasks.

The advanced noticing skills of Brother Lawrence were remarkable and remain inspiring. It's easy to imagine Lawrence noticing so intently that he is oblivious to the sound of banging pots or his cobbler's hammer. As astonishing as his devotion to participating in God's presence may seem to us, Lawrence didn't consider his orientation to God to be a burden. It was simply the fabric of his everyday life, and he felt that practicing the presence was an attainable devotion anyone could engage in. Lawrence's letters reveal how the love of God, his "King," humbled him. In one letter he stated that, upon placing his inequities before God, his King "full of goodness and mercy, lovingly embraces me, seats me at his table, waits on me himself, gives me the keys to his treasures."[11] Recognizing the gravity of God's love, Lawrence responded with a life of loving devotion and advised those who sought his counsel to do the same.

At our distance from Lawrence, ours lives seem wholly different than his. Lawrence was part of a monastic community that oriented all of their activities around established times for contemplative prayer. The rhythms of our twenty-first century lives revolve around activities like working, studying, parenting, and potentially around bingeing on the latest movie streaming, video game or social media fetish. If we choose to make such a distinction between a seventeen-century friar and, say, a twenty-first century soft-ware engineer, then we're missing the essence of Lawrence's example. The focus of Lawrence's prayer time, and the focus of his work time, were one and the same. The good abbot Beauford put it this way:

> [Brother Lawrence said] that it is a big mistake to think that the period of mental prayer should be different from any other. We must be just as closely united with God during our activities as we are during our times of prayer.[12]

The noticing field of engagement is level across all eras. Noticing isn't something we schedule around commitments; it's a life orientation that flows through all commitments. If God's love isn't part-time, then why should noticing be an occasional sideline? Our quest and Lawrence's quest share the same focus and are driven by the same mechanism. The focus is God, and the mechanism is choice: once we notice that we have noticed, orientating our lives to God is a conscious choice. How about that; Brother Lawrence is just like any other passenger in our Noticing Utility Vehicle. At the next rest stop let's all chip in for a *"God Loves! Lawrence Notices!"* bumper sticker.

One of the peculiar things about our noticing trek is that our journey isn't mapped out like other intrepid adventurer quests. There is no atlas that covers the terrain of open-hearted noticing. Instead, we set our course by following the same intangible compass that guided Brother Lawrence's pursuit. There's an orientation that propels our quest participation. Noticing is adventurous and requires real courage. Though, even with these traits, noticing exploits are generally devoid of heroic Hollywood guts and glory stereotypes. I guess that's why Brother Lawrence would never be cast in the leading role of a classic adventure thriller. I don't mean the ankle-deep superhero plots that currently pass for epic adventure stories (and excuses for theme parks). When I think *classic* adventure, my mind drifts to enduring action novels like *Treasure Island*. Robert Louis Stevenson certainly wasn't plotting to launch a new theme park or a line of action figures when he wrote it. Don't let these period sensibilities fool you. While Stevenson may have ignored the licensing of spin-off merchandise, he didn't ignore what really mattered in his story: *Treasure Island* has a map. It's not the kind of map that plots out highways and warns people which routes have tolls. It's the kind of map where **X** marks the hiding place of a buried treasure chest.

If you have ever read *Treasure Island*, or a similar treasure map story, you know that no one follows their map just to ogle a treasure chest. It's never a matter of adventurers seeking the satisfaction of admiring the chest's design and construction. If a writer wants to top the New York Times pirate best seller list, they simply can't go overboard with fanciful descriptions of an unearthed treasure chest. For example, in the first draft of this book, I included this description:

The trunk was a handsome domed chest constructed with interlocking Brazilian olivewood slats stunningly preserved with linseed oil. The heavy fittings were forged iron, and surgeon-precise stitching adorned the chest's rugged leather straps. *Ahoy*, there be exotic woodwork!

My editor, sensing that our adventure tale was unlikely to appeal to woodworking pirates, quickly scuttled this with her red pen. "Enough already! Nobody who reads about bucca-neers and buried gold gives a hoot about the box; it's the treasure inside that matters." She was right: at their core, treasure seeking adventure stories are about the *discovery* of extraordinary riches. Even provocative characters, like Long John Silver and Blackbeard, get bumped from the limelight when its time to open a treasure chest. The climax of a seafaring chest quest thrillingly revolves around the finding and unveiling of incalculable riches. That's a point worth pondering on our journey. We may not have a map, but aren't we seeking the richness of God's love – a treasure we value above all other riches? This is an adventure conundrum. If we don't have a map with **X** marking the location of God's love, where do we dig to find it?

For some historical insight, let's check out a man who, like Brother Lawrence, started out as a soldier before noticing something more important. Iñigo López de Oñaz y Loyola (1491-1556) came from a family of minor nobility in Spain's northern Basque region. He is better known as Ignatius of Loyola, the co-founder and first Superior General of the *Society of Jesus* – the Jesuits. Ignatius wrote numerous documents and letters that give us insight into his noticing skills. Out of his concern to help others develop spiritual attentiveness and openness to God, he crafted a course of spiritual exercises consisting of prayers and meditations. Over the course of many years his own life was a laboratory in which he formulated and refined these tools.

Ignatius also left behind an astonishingly honest journal of personal reflections. It is a record of the emotional highs and

lows of his spiritual journey while serving as the head of the
Jesuit community in Rome. We get a clear understanding of
what fueled Ignatius' demanding educational and humanitar-
ian work, from this journal entry, dated Monday, March 3,
1544.

> In the customary prayer at four o'clock, with great
> devotion, without any movements or disturbances, and
> with some heaviness of the head. I did not venture to get
> up for Mass, but went back to sleep. Getting up later at
> eight, feeling very dull, but neither ill nor well, with no
> one to commend myself to. Afterwards, turning rather to
> Jesus at the preparatory prayer in my room, I felt there a
> slight movement to devotion, and a desire to weep, with
> satisfaction of soul and great confidence in Jesus, being
> drawn to hope in the Most Holy Trinity. Entering the
> chapel and overwhelmed with a great devotion to the
> Most Holy Trinity, with very increased love and intense
> tears, without seeing the Persons distinctly ... but
> perceiving in one luminous clarity a single Essence, I was
> drawn entirely to Its love ....[13]

This reflection makes plain just how open and attentive
Ignatius was to the presence of God. His revealing words
illuminate how he was "entirely drawn" to the love of God.

As fully as Ignatius' journal casts light on his delight in the
love of God, his standing as a notice-master for the ages is
cemented in his correspondence. A letter from 1551 addressing
the spiritual development of Jesuit scholastics is particularly
insightful. In this letter Ignatius advised that scholastics
"should practice the seeking of God's presence in all things, in
their conversations, their walks, in all that they see, taste, hear,
understand, and in all their actions, since God's divine majesty
is truly in all things by his presence, power, and essence."[14]

This advice is strongly associated with Ignatius, and *finding God in all things* remains a cornerstone of Jesuit spirituality.

It's easy to see why we've run into Brother Lawrence and Ignatius Loyola on our notice quest. They're, well … noticeable. Colleagues and strangers alike recognized that Lawrence and Ignatius were the real deal. That's why influential people sought them out for advice during their lifetimes. Their lives pointed to the love of God that they strived to be open to. In the course of everyday life Lawrence and Ignatius consciously sought God's presence in all things. In a way, they so finely developed the discipline of orienting everyday life to God that they left a unique type of map for us to follow. How about that? When we look at pointers like Lawrence and Ignatius, we can see that our noticing journey – which didn't appear to have a map – actually has some wonderful paths etched out for it. The open-hearted disciplines of Lawrence and Ignatius really are more like foot paths than proper maps, but in a real sense, they're even closer to treasure maps. There is no singular bold X to mark the location of God's treasured love. Then again, isn't "seeking God in all things" just another way to acknowledge that we're surrounded by bold Xs? Thanks Lawrence, and thanks to you too, Ignatius. I propose, fellow questers, that if we ever establish a Mount Rushmore for influential noticers, Lawrence and Ignatius get chiselled in. In the meantime, we better clear some space on our bumper for a "seek the presence of God in all things" sticker. Maybe we'll decorate it with a few million Xs.

When we stop to sort out our bumper sticker requirements, we can switch up the Noticing Utility Vehicle seating assignments. I know from personal experience that everyone needs a window seat from time to time. Most questers want to know where they're headed, and a window seat is the place to be when you're trying to read road signs. We're well into our long-haul journey. That means we've already seen plenty of road signs, played too many license plate games, and have heard volumes of stories. Can we squeeze in one more tale? Yes, we're nine chapters in and story fatigue is setting in, but fight it off if you can ... I feel a story coming on.

When it comes to needing a window seat, I really do have some firsthand experience. You see, long before I started any serious noticing, I logged a lot of road miles as a musician. Most of the time I played in rock or pop bands, but on a few occasions I rode the range with country bands. Playing in country bars is ideal if you have a taste for songs steeped in broken-hearted drama. During one road trip I played with a country singer named Don. It is no exaggeration to say that Don was a high drama connoisseur. He was a sometimes truck driver who had done a short stretch for kicking a police officer precisely where he oughtn't. His record, and his tough demeanour, made him the picture of the (then current) country outlaw movement. Don introduced me to a swath of lonesome unrequited love songs. This genre has a long history in the country fold: old songs like *I Know You're Married but I Love You Still* by Dolly Parton and Porter Wagoner, and newer pop-country tunes like Taylor Swift's *Teardrops on My Guitar*. These "I can't have your love" songs have a sobbing sub-genre that specialises in mourning over lost love. Don sang a bunch of these too. He favoured the standards like *He Stopped Loving Her Today* by George Jones, and Patsy Cline's rendition of *Crazy*, which Willie Nelson penned. These songs just might be the pinnacle of lost love lament. In one of the seedier bars I played, I saw a low soul plug quarters into a jukebox for hours playing nothing but lost love songs. If I had been drinking a beer, you can bet I would have shed a few tears in it.

I'll admit to learning a few things about life in country bars, but I never really felt at home in them. The music can be heartbreaking, but it can also be celebratory. One thing is certain, country tunes drive home the truth that love makes the world go around. Love is a precious gift that drives our choices and priorities. We have to take chances in love, because all love must be offered before it can be accepted. Songs aren't needed to tell us that unrequited love is painful; we know this. Love that is offered and not accepted bounces back like a piercing sting to the heart. Ouch.

Love and trust go together hand-in-hand. When one of those hands lets go, the loss of love has the loss of trust imbedded in it. Even when our noticing skills are at their weakest, we all notice the loss of love. Taking a chance on love and coming up short toughens our hearts. In the aftermath our reflex is to shy away from trusting in love. Have you ever noticed though, that even when we're shying away from love, God isn't? The love of God is constantly on offer. It is different than the human love we take a chance on. God's love is extended to us, which means the accepting is up to us. Our love for God is never unrequited, because God has always taken the first step by offering divine love to us.

There will never be songs about God's unrequited love, nor will there be any about losing God's love. The love of God cannot be lost, though it can be tossed. Our freedom allows us to reject God's love, but even willful rejection doesn't erase God's love. God's self-offer is constant, just as God's presence is constant and God's love is constant. Remember that God's self-offer is an invitation to *all* humankind (yep, we're all in on this). As long as we live, by grace, our names are engraved on God's invitation list. On our quest we've peeked at God's self-offer from many directions; it is high time we peeked at it through the eyes of love. We have no higher standard than the love of God. We have no greater offer than the love that is given so that we may accept it. Yes, a person may, in the totality of their life, choose to reject God's loving self-offer. We have to see this rejection for what it is. When a person rejects God, *they* are choosing to say, "God, my love is lost to you."

God ultimately fulfills our heart's desire, even if our desire is to be apart from God. This is why the freedom to accept love is one of God's most profound gifts to humankind.

We have covered a lot of ground on this stage of our journey. That's to be expected when you're taking stock of the love of God. There is no other love that shines so big and bright. Yet, there is also no other love that so subtly and quietly keeps us company with its presence. God's love overwhelms the night like a symphony of neon, and whispers love in the stillness of each sunset. All this love has me thinking; where did we put down Ignatius' footpath map? Let's park the Noticing Utility Vehicle and take a stroll on Brother Lawrence's trail. After the twists and turns of noticing trash bins, and pointing to mystery, grace, hope and a whole lot of love, let's spend our last chapter contemplating what we've noticed.

10

Walk On
(and Fill in the Blanks)

Eventually, we all have to learn to walk. There is no way around this; each of us must learn to walk. By the way, this has nothing to do with being able-bodied. Nor does it have much to do with the tentative steps that babies make when they decide that verticality is where the action is. The walking I'm talking is the opposite of running, and it's all in the mind. We live in a mile-a-minute (or kilometer-a-kilosecond) world that emphasises speed. This penchant for quickness isn't a disease that sneaks up on us in our twilight years. On the contrary, it begins at birth. Do you know a single woman who would prefer a long-drawn-out labour to a "barely made it to the hospital" quick step? We're hardly home from the hospital before the speed judgments start: we may be deemed *quick-witted*, or cast in with the *slow kids*. Soon after, parents jockey to secure a pole position for their toddling tykes in pre-preschool "head start" programs. Then it's on to elementary school where physical education classes typically require kids to run the hundred-yard dash. There are two reasons for this: explaining a 91.44 metres trot is awkward, and teachers and kids alike are absurdly acclimatized to speed.

In a sneaky way, our societal behaviour is geared to propelling us along the fast track. You know the drill: fast food, fast and furious entertainment, and fast internet (or we'll quickly get cranky). In adulthood, it's all too easy for us to unwittingly perpetuate the speed cycle. Parents, have you ever told your child, "You can't go out to play until you finish your dinner"? If that doesn't speed up vegetable inhalation, nothing will. In the teenage years this turbo-push is aided and abetted at every turn. For a prime example, look no further than those sketchy amusement park ride operators bent on accelerating the velocity of youth. Essentially, their job is to blast pulsing music and ask, "Do you want to go faster?" Then, when their riders dutifully scream, they are rewarded with … more speed.

Nobody knows the slowest time ever posted for a Boston marathon, or an Olympic downhill skiing event. Do you know who drove the slowest Indianapolis 500, the famous car race held annually at Indianapolis Motor *Speedway* in *Speedway*, Indiana? Neither do I, but whoever it is, they're my favourite driver. I'm a firm believer that slow is much trickier than fast these days. That's because in our velocity mindedness, faster has became synonymous with better. Okay, I do agree that faster *is* better when it comes to ambulance response time and root canal procedures. When it comes to everyday noticing, though, fast gets a failing grade. How can the pointers around us effectively point if our minds blur by them at top speed? Questers, there is no way around this; each of us must learn to walk.

Oh boy, it's muttering time again. The moment we parked the Noticing Utility Vehicle it became evident that some of us aren't seasoned walkers. Yes, I heard that remark about walking being beneath real intrepid adventurers. And whoever said "nobody puts walking on their adventure bucket list," has obviously never perused an issue of *Walking, Country Walking, Women's Walking,* or *Great Walks* at their local magazine stand. Bucket lists aren't all about African safaris, swimming with dolphins, and bungee jumping. Just look at Palle Huld, the Danish Boy Scout who, in 1928, pulled off an *Around the World in Eighty Days* adventure in just forty-six days. Huld, who was

Each of us must learn to walk

then only fifteen years old, won a newspaper competition held to mark the centenary of author Jules Verne. The prize was a re-enactment of the voyage undertaken by Phileas Fogg, the main character in Verne's *Around the World in Eighty Days* adventure novel. Staying true to the propulsion options of Fogg's era, Huld by-passed speedy aeroplanes and travelled only by land and sea.[1] He successfully circumnavigated the globe, and visited England, Canada, Japan, the Soviet Union, Poland and Germany along the way. Huld was a real adventurer *and* a conscious noticer. When he triumphantly returned to Denmark, Huld wrote a book about his trek (published in English as *A Boy Scout Around the World*)[2]. This account of his adventures was just shy of two hundred noticing pages long. There can be no doubt that Huld was a teenage Danish Boy Scout who noticed, *and was noticed*.

Among those who have noticed Huld are avid fans of the popular character Tin Tin. Some tintinologists claim that the young fictional adventurer Tin Tin, introduced by the Belgian cartoonist Hergé the year after Huld's trek, bears a striking resemblance to the red haired Huld. For his part, Huld, who passed away in 2010, claimed to have never read a Tin Tin book. He did, however, confirm that completing his adventure crossed an item off his personal bucket list. In Huld's words, "It was a big dream … I wanted to see the world. My red hair, a rare thing in Denmark, made me stand out."[3] Three cheers for the red-headed teen who chose ocean liner and train propulsion over the blur of aeroplane rapidity. In doing so, he noticed that there is a world of noticing to be noticed.

Huld's real life Tin Tin experience is proof that allowing our minds to walk at a noticing pace doesn't mean living at a snail's pace. Just look at those diehard adventurers who maintain their noticing momentum by living in homes on wheels. They're like fancy Noticing Utility Vehicles with comfy beds and propane gas appliances. Still, even camper van and motorhome enthusiasts eventually have to park their palaces and walk. I witnessed this firsthand in 1985, during a summer spent two hundred kilometers north of the Arctic Circle. I was in the tiny town of Inuvik, in Canada's North West Territories. Don't ask why; it's a long story steeped in romance that would require a whole other book. The point is, the Arctic was a peculiar place to meet a Texan crossing things off his bucket list. You see, this bucket fellow and his wife drove a camper all the way from Texas to Inuvik. That's roughly a 6,700 kilometer drive (a.k.a. 4,150 tall Texan miles). The couple accomplished this by travelling on some of the worst northern rubble that ever disgraced the name "highway." When they arrived in town, I asked the fellow why he made the ridiculously long and dangerous drive. His answer was simply that he had always wanted to drive to the end of the line. That's exactly what he thought he had done. At the time, Inuvik was as far north as he could drive – it was literally the end of the road.

If you're wondering what Texan bucket lists have to do with noticing, I'll tell you the plain facts. When this Texas wanderer stopped at the end of the road, he hadn't really crossed a line off his bucket list. What he mistook for the end of the line was, in truth, a line that does not end – he still had to get out and walk. Yes, he had exhausted the length of the thoroughfare; his wheels could go no further. He had arrived at the point that separates noticing through a windshield and noticing on a footpath ... just like we have. When we exhaust the velocity of our twenty-first century lives and get serious about noticing ... we have to do it at a walking pace. Again, there is no way around this: the mind of each and every notice-quester must learn to walk. This is why we parked the Noticing Utility Vehicle. Noticing is a mental footpath, akin to the presence paths of Lawrence and Ignatius. Like the Texan, we can cover a lot of ground in comfort, but we'll miss the pointers if our rushing around reduces them to blurs. At the end of the day, not all lines on a bucket list are created equal. Once we dismount the velocity express of life and let our minds walk, we discover that we never reach the end of the noticing line. Noticing is the line on your bucket list that never gets crossed off … and that is noticeably wonderful.

While we're still together, we'll spend a little time on our footpath discussing everyday things. All this talk about adventurers has me wondering about the things that *don't* turn up on a *once-in-a-lifetime* bucket list. I propose that we make a different kind of list; one that includes the everyday things in a noticer's everyday life. That means we're compiling something like a *thrice-in-a-daytime* bucket list, except ours should be smaller than a bucket … more like a beach pail.[4] Buckets are used for heavy work like milking cows and mucking out stables. Beach pails are used for pleasure. Even so, each one can hold more grains of sand than we can possibly count (like a pail of unquantifiable teensy tiny pointers). It's settled; ours is a *pail* list.

Let's think back over our journey together and contemplate what should be on our notice-quester's pail list. For starters – before anything goes on our list – we need to leave some blank spaces. Yes, that is an odd way to start a list. However, if we have noticed anything, we've noticed that EVERYTHING POINTS TO GOD. From the get-go, our revamping of the Kevin Bacon *degrees of separation* game handily demonstrated this truth. Given that *everything* is quite a lot of things, we better leave some room for unexpected eureka entries along the path. If you're like me, you probably never expected to stumble onto things like pointing trash bins. Having so surprisingly stumbled, I now keep my mind open for *UPTs*. That stands for *unanticipated pointy things*, and they can pile up into quite a list all on their own.

For the next entry, let's recall the horizon comparison broached a while back in chapter two. The horizon is a constant reminder of the way all material, cognitive and sensory pointers refer to God. If we picture the horizon as a backdrop, we see how its presence illustrates our pre-conscious orientation towards God that Rahner called pre-apprehension (or *Vorgriff*). Terminology aside, imagining that God is in our field of vision, as the backdrop beyond all that we apprehend, helps brings this theory to life. Whether we're conscious of it or not, the horizon – like God – is constantly present in everyday life. The horizon is a great reminder of God's presence, so it belongs on our pail list: *notice the horizon*.

As long as we're on the subject of visual prompts, we always have the option to add our own symbolic reminders to our everyday path. This is a delightful idea that anyone can size to suit their living space and aesthetic sensibilities. Reminders can be big and bold, like the gilded paintings venerated as icons in the Eastern Orthodox branch of our family tree. Going the other way, we can select a reminder pointer that's as portable and low key as a bonsai tree on our breakfast table. Noticing the symbols that are physically present in our lives, reminds us that Jesus physically joined us as the real-symbol and real presence of God. Of course, the word *symbol* can be stretched in a lot of directions. Knowing this, our pail list needs an entry with suitable elasticity: *Notice material signs of a spiritual world.* That covers a lot of ground and gives each of us the chance to tailor symbols to fit our personal sensibilities.

I'm sensing there's some "if only it was so easy" head scratching going on. We want our everyday pail list to be realistic, but so far it just has a couple of reminder tips. I hear you, and I've logged a few head scratching grimaces myself. After all, if noticing was as easy as just opening our eyes and remembering to notice, we wouldn't need a list. Let's have a show of hands: How many of us would say "easy" is the word that best describes a typical day? Not too many; most of us live with a scarcity of *easy.* To one degree or another we're all preoccupied with everyday routine work and worries. There are even days when meanspirited events keep our heads down. At times like these, who is raising their eyes to take in the horizon? Can we really be expected to notice a miniscule bonsai tree beside our Corn Flakes in the morning? Is our pail list just an artificial exercise of putting smiley face stickers on our otherwise dull and dreary to-do lists? Oddly enough, the best way to sort this is to count how many times the words "conscious" and its derivatives have appeared in this book so far. I'll save you the trouble, the answer is a whopping forty-five times. That's a repetitive hint that the noticing we've been batting around isn't a garden variety open-my-eyes-and-see noticing. It's life-orientation intentional heads-up conscious and curious wonderment noticing. Throughout our journey we've been concerned with what we do *after noticing that we have noticed.* Ours is not a flip-of-the-coin happenstance outing; intrepid adventuring is an eyes-open conscious business.

Our journey is real fabric of life stuff, so we have to accept that we're not going to be noticing-Einsteins everyday. I know that my bulb can be as dim as anyone's, and that nobody escapes the burden of bulb burn out. Even that brainy quester Rahner succumbed to down days and acknowledged that we all have periods of low luminosity. Coaxing out the truth, Rahner said, "Be frank. Are there not times when we feel oppressed by the gloom, the meanness, the petty egoism, the spite, the gossip, and all the things that make up our routine?"[5] This is a grim, but true, assessment. All of the noticing prompts in the world mean nothing if we forget that we are equipped to notice the constant self-offer of God. Conscious noticing breaks the gloom and lifts our eyes to the horizon. It is the fuel that sparks our engagement with the everyday signs of God's presence. If our daily reminders can help keep God's self-offer front and center in our lives, well, what more can we ask of a pail list?

Taking everyday notice of the constant offer of God elevates our inevitable routines. As Rahner put it: "It is certain that everyday routine exists and we cannot escape most of it. Even the saints yawn sometimes, and have to shave."[6] Given this certainty, there's no reason to believe that the ebb and flow that characterizes our day-to-day routines won't also be evident in our spiritual lives. Conscious noticing can restore our spiritual equilibrium by taking a page from Brother Lawrence's playbook. The general muddle we get into when trying to reconcile what we perceive as the ebb and flow of God's presence, wasn't Lawrence's style at all. As we've seen, his practice of a "general and loving awareness of God" didn't distinguish between divine nearness and distance. We ran into Lawrence in chapter nine, but his thinking was already simmering beneath our handling of the *hiddenness* of God way back in chapter four. There, we confronted how odd it is to search God out when God seems remote, yet knowing all the while that God is constantly present. This makes us anxious even though creation itself continuously points to God's attending presence. From time to time this is going to concern all of us, so we'd better jot down a strategy on our pail list. Here's the plan: we peek over Brother Lawrence's shoulder and borrow the wording on his list. Got it; it says, "practice the presence of God." Feel free to mix Lawrence's words around to suit your personal taste. You can capture the essence with *notice the constancy of God*, or maybe, *listen for God's constant presence*. Sometimes analogous language is the way to go. Talking about God generally means stretching our words, and *listening* is the very picture of an attentive heart yearning for God. Think about how you want to describe your conscious attentiveness to God, and tag it on your list.

One of the great things about slow walking on the noticing path is that it fits well with the pace of mystery. Objectively, who can say whether mystery has a speed? It's a weird idea, but I think you know what I mean. It just doesn't feel like there's anything fast about mystery. Profoundly deep matters, like divine mystery, don't rush by. Perhaps it's more accurate to say that we slowly amble through mystery. We're always (and will always be) a step behind, so it feels like mystery is just ahead, slowly leading us deeper into ... enigmatic _____. I'll let you fill in the last word for yourself. Not surprisingly, you'll have to go deeper into mystery to find it. Whatever words we fill our blanks with, we can't simply add a line to our pail list that says *notice divine mystery*. Let's face it: that's just another way to describe *every* line on our list. I vote that we go right to the heart of the matter and pen in *sacramental orientation*. That's a tidy way of saying that everyday we are oriented to encounter divine mystery. It's an orientation to the encounters through which we engage the loving extravagance of God's ever-present self-offer. Besides, an invitation to the unknown adds a little spice to any list.

Sacramental orientation isn't a loner; it always keeps company. All great pairings (like peanut butter and jelly or Batman and Robin), seem to flourish in faithful tandem. I suppose that's why we can only develop a sacramental orientation to God's presence by embracing faith. Faith and sacramental orientation are a dynamic duo. When I bring up faith, I'm not referring to a trusting confidence in God, or a reassurance that God's revelation is reliable. These are fine and good to be sure, but they fall short of the open-hearted leap that constitutes faith. Louis Dupré, who we checked in with in chapter three, has offered up some valuable insights into the nature of faith. In Dupré's assessment, "Faith is never an immediate feeling or emotion. It is the awareness of a transcendent dimension to all the experiences of life, the affirmation of a deeper reality underlying the obvious appearances."[7] Awareness of the spiritual reality underlying our world is like a door open just enough to allow a crack of light through. This glimmer of light introduces possibilities so startling that it captures our human imagination. Some may call this glimmer enticing, but I think *inviting* is a more apt description. God's self-offer does not coerce humanity. God's offer of participation now, and eternally, is extended to our human freedom. It is offered so that we may accept it for what it is, and not because we are fooled by a false enticement. Christian faith matures though participation in God's spiritual reality, in our everyday earthly reality. That is how faith emerges as something more than trust and belief. Faith is a state of active participation in God's self-offer, which is why sacramental orientation and faith go hand-in-hand. Christian faith has eyes to see God's spiritual reality, because sacramental orientation points us towards the glimmer of spiritual light seeping into our lives.

At this stage of our quest, can you imagine noticing without participating? After surveying even a few corners of God's loving expression to us, the notion of not participating seems downright odd. Well, there's the rub: we know a thing or two about being downright odd. In a world of participating possibilities, we tend to veer towards sedentary observance. Yup, we know we're spectacular spectators. We'll watch just about anything provided we can stay couch-spud comfortable. Sometimes our devotion to spectating devolves into absurd contradiction. For example: in theory, the concept of scripting fake confrontations between people acting out before cameras – and then calling it *reality* television – is a complete nonstarter. However, if you broadcast the results as an alternative to active participation, you can attract a million couch-comfy spectators. At times it appears that participation needs a crafty synopsis to attract more participants. You know, like the brief blurbs that describe YouTube "skateboarding cat shows off" videos.[8] If that's what it takes, I nominate this blurb written by Rahner for our participation synopsis:

History is not just a play in which God puts himself on the stage and creatures are merely what is performed; the creature is a real co-performer in this humano-divine drama of history.[9]

Wow, that's a whole lot more interesting than cats on wheels. God's presence is an invitation to be co-present with God – a co-performer participant in human history. The unscripted and genuine reality of participating is a huge component of God's self-offer. This belongs on our pail list. You can write in Rahner's synopsis quote if you like; it's a keeper. I'm going to write in another shorthand reduction: *Participate with God as a co-performer.* That will be my daily cue to notice how great co-billing with God is. If you think that "co-performer" sounds a bit presumptuous, I suggest re-reading the scriptural accounts of the covenants God has made with his people.[10] The loving invitation to be God's supporting cast has *always* been about co-performing and cooperating with God.

Our pail list is shaping up nicely. Adding to our everyday content list reminds me of those ingredient labels that manufacturers put on food products. Usually when I read the label on processed food, I have two reactions: consternation and puzzlement. The consternation comes from quantifying the volume of sugar, sweeteners, salt and fat that are clogging up my favourite foods (and possibly my arteries). My puzzlement is aroused by the unfamiliar additive names that may, or may not, have connections with a shadowy dietary underworld we have no access to. Frankly, I don't understand the terminology, and I have no idea why artificial colouring is numbered. Is Red Dye #2 somehow less desirable than Red Dye #9? Maybe the dye industry is populated by golfers, and the lower numbers are better? I can't make sense of it – which may just be how the golfers want to play this thing. On the pail list front this isn't a factor. Sure, God loves golfers, but the notice path includes folks from all walks of life. I'm confident that our pail list has nothing on it to evoke feelings of consternation. However, any label or list that includes *participation* in its ingredients may bring on twinges of puzzlement.

Thinking back over our journey, we've already kicked the term participation around a bit. We've hit on numerous examples of participation in God's constant offer to humankind. In fact, we've even got an umbrella term that will help demystify *participation*. With this in mind, I've augmented my *participation* entry on our pail list. It now reads: *Participate with God as a co-performer (Agent of Grace).* This is a superbly compact way to spell out a world of participation possibilities. We did discuss our role as agents *en route* in the Noticing Utility Vehicle. Nonetheless, it is worth revisiting while we walk. "Grace" describes God's self-revealing activity. This means that God's self-communicating presence, in Jesus, in the Holy Spirit, and in all of the myriad of ways God addresses the offer of salvation to us, are gifts of God's grace. It also means that the gifts and capacities that God bestows on us are grace, because they facilitate our recognition of God's self-offer. God's grace in our lives is always good news. And because grace permeates our lives, we can participate in God's grace. We can act as agents who communicate the love of God and the hope we have through God.

Our participation possibilities are endless, which means they won't all fit on a concise pail list. Heck, even the *Love of God and Love of Neighbour* possibilities we explored earlier would, on their own, turn our list into a hefty volume. With this in mind, I'll stick to three short words to help clarify our participation role: *Agents of Grace.* For those agents who would rather capture the enormous scope of grace with one of Rahner's keen insights, here's a gem: "God is exit and entrance, beginning and end, center and meaning. Everything belongs to him, everything proclaims his glory, everything is subject to his grace."[11] As is usual with Rahner, this quote is too long for a bumper sticker. Nonetheless, when I next run across the Noticing Utility Vehicle, I might just paint this adaptation on the side doors:

EVERYTHING BELONGS TO GOD

EVERYTHING PROCLAIMS GOD'S GLORY

EVERYTHING IS SUBJECT TO GOD'S GRACE

Reading these three *everything* statements back-to-back, I'm struck by how familiar they look. Hey, do these statements remind you of the day we first met up in chapter one? Whoa, I'm experiencing a hybrid eureka-*déjà vu*. This all seems so familiar, yet somehow, I sense that it's brand new. We came together as a questing group about the time I dished up the pointing trash bin story. Now, after ten chapters, we're face-to-face with three *everything* statements that spell out our launch point all over again:

EVERYTHING POINTS TO GOD.

I sense you're perilously close to stepping off the noticing path and waving the rest of us off: "Thanks for the quest but it's time to go – this is where I came in." Hold on just a pointy-noticing minute! Let's take stock of where we are on our journey. Some of you think we've passed Go, collected two-hundred dollars, and are now on the repeat round to pointers we've already seen. All the while, I'm wondering what to do with that eureka-*déjà vu* thing that feels so familiar. It's as if we've lost the plot and have forgotten every morsel of questing that we've communally quested together. Quick, let's pull out our pail list and get our bearings. Hmmm … Here it is:

- *Notice the horizon*
- *Notice material signs of a spiritual world·*
- *Notice divine mystery*

So far, so good. These entries all remind us to notice things that are constant. The horizon is always with us. It's always beyond our immediate grasp, but when we look for it, we find the horizon is always present. Seek and you shall find – that's the horizon to a tee. Even if I'm sitting in a dark movie theatre, I know that the horizon is still constantly there. Yes, even in the darkness, we know that the horizon is hanging around. The same holds true for material signs that prompt us to sense the underlying spiritual world. I don't just mean the obvious ones, like where Michelangelo got carried away doodling on that ceiling in the Sistine Chapel. I'm also thinking about summer sunflowers, stained glass windows, the framed rendering of Psalm 145 in my home, and the praises I've read on countless gravestones. Really, what could be more consistently in our faces than the vast sea of visual pointers that surround us? When it comes to divine mystery, we're never short of visual reminders. Then there's the intangible and invisible reminders. When God's presence presses on my heart I don't need symbols or keepsakes to illuminate God's constant self-offer. Neither snow nor rain nor heat nor gloom of night stays the constant grace of God. Okay, these entries are clear enough. Next on the pail list, we have:

- *Conscious attentiveness to God (Practice the presence of God)*
- *Participate with God as a co-performer (Agent of Grace)*

These entries are the other side of the noticing coin. Now our whole eureka-*déjà vu*-old-and-new conundrum makes perfect sense. When we thought the notice path was looking familiar, it was. That was the constant *unchanging offer of God* part of our notice quest. The flip side of this is the *everyday new and uncharted territory* we encounter when we do our participation-part. What makes us notice questers is our active participation in the constant offer of God. It's entirely up to us to be attentive to God. We are invited to be co-performers, but it's up to us to spread the love, hope and promise of God's self-offer. We can find our way through questing's ongoing newness. After all, Jesus has made it abundantly clear what attentiveness and participation can look like in human history. Noticing the revelation of Jesus in history is at the core of noticing the *hows* and *whys* of participating today, and tomorrow, and everyday. Seeing both sides of the notice/participate coin clears up a lot of questions. In particular, it makes sense of the first entry on our pail list. It's truly open-ended, so I've left it for last:

- _____

- _____

When the whole pail list idea came up, I was kind of pushy about the first entry. In fact, I insisted that "before anything goes on our list, we need to leave some blank spaces." Above you see a couple of those aforementioned spaces. The grace of God is beyond measure, and noticing is never passive. That's a quester's recipe for the mysterious and unexpected to cross our noticing path. Wow, this pail list was a great idea. I think we've got our bearings set. That's good news, because we're getting close to the beginning of the next path. Soon we'll be exchanging high-fives and scattering in different directions.

Thanks for questing with me and giving me space to tell the occasional story. On first glance, the idea of noticing may not have seemed like much. The possibility of sharing an entire book about noticing ... preposterous. Still, everything in our lives has a beginning, and noticing is no exception. We all have to notice the constant offer of God for ourselves. More precisely: it's essential that we *begin* noticing. Then, noticing that we have noticed, the quest begins in earnest with life transforming questions, like:

- Given that God's self-offer is continuous, shouldn't we desire our noticing to be continuous?

- Shouldn't this desire shape our entire life focus - the very orientation of our being?

And so, we engage the constant offer of God, noticing anew again and again. My engagements, whether in my own Noticing Utility Vehicle or along our shared noticing path, have reoriented my life orientation. Once I would have agreed with René Descartes' assessment that "I think, therefore I am." Now, I say that *I notice, therefore I point.* By the way, you're doing a fine job of pointing too.

If you have persevered through this journey wondering how God can possibly invite us *all* to participate as co-performers, the answer to your questions is: grace. Along this line, Rahner expressed that "Christianity is indeed an optimism about human beings such as only God could conceive."[12] We do not see ourselves as God lovingly sees us. God can offer God's self in whatever manner, or to whatever degree, that God desires. We cannot fathom God's loving generosity. God loves actively, constantly, presently, invitingly, and eternally. Any glimpse we gain of God's divine mystery is a glimpse of love.

The apostle Paul is always good for a quote. That's likely because he was a feisty speaker with no shortage of wisdom. His was the kind of wisdom that crossed all boundaries, and with time has become part of the fabric of modern life. Whether you attend church, or prefer to attend to anything but church come Sunday morning, you've heard Paul quoted. Oh yes you have! I'm thinking of a particular quote. In fact, if Paul released a *Greatest Quotes* album, this might just be side one, track one. I'm referring to Paul's renowned description of love. A wedding ceremony staple, it goes like this:

> Love is patient; love is kind; love is not envious or boastful or arrogant or rude. It does not insist on its own way; it is not irritable or resentful; it does not rejoice in wrongdoing, but rejoices in the truth. It bears all things, believes all things, hopes all things, endures all things. (1 Corinthians 13:5-7)

Yes, this is wonderful, and classic, and apropos for weddings … but that's not why I bring it up. I'm shining a light on this gem to preface another confession. That's right, I began this book with a confession, and I'm closing with another. Here goes: I must confess that when I hear this excerpt from Paul's first letter to the church in Corinth, this bit just drifts by me. If I was at your wedding and you played Paul's *Greatest Quotes* album, I didn't walk away humming this passage (sorry, it was a lovely service). No, it is the three words that appear immediately *after* this quote that always stick with me. These are the words that I always walk away humming: "Love never ends" (1 Corinthians 13:8).

The pointers we notice in the course of each and every day hum this, whisper this, shout this, and engrave this truth across the sky: "Love never ends." God's love is eternal; it never ends. By grace, God's loving self-communication and offer of salvation is constant in our lives. Let us notice this, so that we too, can be pointers worthy of noticing.

And so, we come to the parting juncture of this leg of our quest. We've followed our path to an end that is a starting point, and I count such points as precious. If you are wondering why our starting points are precious, I can only respond by flipping back to chapter one, when:

In the Milky Way Galaxy, on the planet Earth, on the west coast of Canada, in the suburbs of Vancouver, one back lane west of the crossroads of Austin Avenue and Schoolhouse Street, in a parking lot at 49^0 14' 58.3"N latitude and $122^0 51' 19.2$"W longitude, I noticed that a garbage bin points to God – because everything points to God. Noticing that I noticed; I recognized my starting point ... and started anew in the never-ending amazement of noticing.

Walk on ....

Notes and Sources

Chapter 1 My Story (or When I Noticed …)

[1] Forbes Agency Council posted this tidbit on August 25, 2017. You can find it here:
forbes.com/sites/forbesagencycouncil/2017/08/25/finding-brand-success-in-the-digital-world/#6cae81a7626e.

[2] This observation from 1955 (sadly) continues to be relevant today. *Surprised by Joy* has appeared in numerous editions over the years. I pulled this quote from:
C S. Lewis, *Surprised by Joy: The Shape of My Early Life* (San Francisco: HarperOne, 2017), 254.

[3] I'm indebted to stalwart cinephile Zachary Williams for providing this example. His brain is a richly stocked depository of motion picture minutiae which should never, under any circumstances, be challenged to a Six Degrees of Separation duel.

[4] I found this bit of truth in a book full of good bits. You can find it too: Anne Lamott, *Bird by Bird: Some Instructions on Writing and Life* (New York: Pantheon Books, 1994), 22.

Chapter 2 Pointers to God (the Visible and the Invisible)

[1] The big numbers on the Hubble price tag can be found on page 32 of the *James Webb Space Telescope Independent Comprehensive Review Panel Final Report*. Peruse it at your leisure:
nasa.gov/pdf/499224main_JWST-ICRP_Report-FINAL.pdf

[2] Check this figure, and other fascinating Ontario Ministry of Heritage, Sport, Tourism and Culture Industries data, here:
mtc.gov.on.ca/en/research/rtp/rtp.shtml

[3] This is from the first verse of Psalm 19. The psalmist, like virtually all authors prior to the late 20th century, uses masculine pronouns to refer to God. There are select cases in this book in

which quotes have been altered by substituting "God" for masculine pronouns. Generally, quotes are reproduced without alteration. Let's agree not to raise a stink and simply acknowledge that God transcends our biological gender classifications, and the English language is gender-neutral deficient in the pronoun department.

[4] Thomas Aquinas, *Summa Contra Gentiles* 3, 49, n. 3 (Bk. 3, Ch. 49, Sec. 3). Again, don't get too hung up on the masculine pronouns; Thomas was a man of his age.

[5] Latin speaking contemporaries called him Aurelius Augustinus, but we'll refer to the Bishop of Hippo simply as Augustine. This quote is an excerpt from: Augustine, *Confessions* 10.9. All excerpts from *Confessions* appear in the Sarah Ruden translation. Augustine, *Confessions* (New York: The Modern Library, 2017).

[6] Augustine, *The Greatness of the Soul* (*De quantitate animae*) 34.77.

[7] Rahner wrote complex academic works, but also a large number of very approachable articles for non-specialists. Amongst this later group there are many homilies which address specific dates in the liturgical calendar of the church. This particular quote is from: Karl Rahner, "Shrove Tuesday," in *The Eternal Year* (Baltimore: Helicon Press, 1964), 55. We'll draw on both Rahner's academic and liturgical contributions as our journey progresses.

[8] Note to potentially litigiously-minded designers of Swedish fibreboard furnishings: imitation är den högsta formen av smicker.

[9] Karl Rahner, "Prayer for Creative Thinkers," in *Theological Investigations* Vol. 8, 130.

[10] Karl Rahner, "Thomas Aquinas: Monk, Theologian and Mystic," in *The Great Church Year* (New York: Crossroads, 1994), 312.

[11] Although his birth name was Giovanni di Fidanza, we know him as St. Bonaventure of Bagnoregio, or simply *Bonaventure*. There is a certain cool factor connected to adopting a single name. Could it be that Bonaventure influenced Elvis, Cher, Sting and Bono?

[12] Bonaventure, *The Journey of the Mind to God* 2.11.
Bonaventure trivia: As a child Bonaventure suffered from a life-threatening bowel-related illness. He recovered and is now acknowledged as the patron saint of bowel disorders.

[13] *The Life of Saint Francis* by Julian of Speyer, in *Francis of Assisi: Early Documents,* Regis J. Armstrong, ed. *(New York: New City Press, 1999-2000),* 399. You can access a wealth of Francis-related information at franciscantradition.org

[14] Augustine, *Confessions* 10.8.

[15] Karl Rahner "The Christian, The Devil and Culture," in *Biblical Homilies* (Freiburg: Herder, 1966), 47.

[16] In his famous work *The City of God* (*De civitate Dei*), Augustine wrote: "For evil is not a positive substance: the loss of good has been given the name 'evil'" (*The City of God* 11.10). This echoes the earlier thinking of the philosopher Plotinus (ca. 204 – 270; see his *Enneads* 3.2.5). Though the influence of Plotinus can be seen in Augustine (particularly his earliest writings), Augustine and Plotinus held fundamentally different ideas about the nature of the Creator. Thomas Aquinas also explores why evil can be understood as an absence of good in *Summa Theologica* Ia, q. 48, art. 1.

[17] Karl Rahner, "If the Heart is Alive it Thinks of God," in *Biblical Homilies,* 152.

Chapter 3 Revelation (and the Art of Mediation)

[1] In this make-believe story, a defunct pop group faces the long-standing reunion question: Will folks pay to see our act without our big-name original member? Sometimes the cash registers ring loudly (Queen, Fleetwood Mac, Pink Floyd), and sometimes they whimper (The Doors of the 21st Century, The New Cars, Genesis with Ray Wilson). Let's face it, some performers need their famous partner(s) to pull it off. After all, who would pay to see Cher without Sonny?

[2] Here's a tip for readers looking to have their marriage proposal announced to the world on a major league baseball scoreboard: go to Pittsburgh. PNC Park, where the Pirates play their home games, is (as of this writing) the cheapest stadium for scoreboard proposals. Dodger Stadium in Los Angeles is by far the most expensive MLB proposal option. You can propose twenty-five times at Yankee Stadium for the cost of just one proposal at Dodger Stadium (or propose sixty-four times in Pittsburgh, the thrifty-romance capital of big league ball).

You can check out your hometown stadium proposal fee here: theknot.com/content/baseball-stadium-proposal-costs (accessed November 7, 2020).

[3] This is drawn from Dupré's book *Symbols of the Sacred*, which contains four insightful essays on symbols. He begins the book by helping readers to distinguish between signs and symbols. You'll find that bit here: Louis Dupré, *Symbols of the Sacred* (Grand Rapids, MI: Eerdmans, 2000), 1.

[4] Louis Dupré, "Of Holy Signs," in *Symbols of the Sacred*, 24.

[5] Officially known as the Orthodox Catholic Church, though commonly, and respectfully, referred to as the Eastern Orthodox Church.

[6] When considering icons, remember our concerns are noticing and the reality of divine presence. There are numerous examples of God the Father being portrayed as a human patriarch figure in both Western art and Eastern iconography, but it is generally understood that the eternal nature of God cannot be visibly rendered like portraiture. Icons depicting Christ depict the human form of Jesus, not the eternal nature of Christ. That's why iconographers often indicate the presence of the Holy Trinity with symbols, like angels, radiance, or haloes. These symbols signify the presence of the unrenderable. If this seems odd to our Western sensibilities, consider it as paralleling the long history of symbolic representations of the Holy Spirit in both Eastern and Western art.

[7] Alexander Schmemann, *For the Life of the World: Sacraments and Orthodoxy* (Crestwood, NY: St. Vladimir's Seminary Press, 1973), 141.

[8] The two periods of heightened tension in the "Iconoclast controversy" run approximately from 726 to 787, and from 814 to 842.

[9] This excerpt appears in Alexander Schmemann, *The Historical Road to Eastern Orthodoxy* (New York: Holt, Rinehart and Wilson, 1963), 203.

[10] Sourced from: Denzinger-Bannwart, *Enchiridon Symbolorun*, 31st edition (Barcelona, 1957), no. 337.

[11] Vladimir Lossky, *The Mystical Theology of the Eastern Church* (Crestwood, NY: St. Vladimir's Seminary Press, 1976), 10. Lossky's use of "energy" refers to the presence and "divine force" of the Holy Spirit.

[12] Vladimir Lossky, *The Mystical Theology of the Eastern Church*, 189.

[13] Martin Luther, *Luther's Works* Vol. 40, ed. Conrad Bergendoff (Philadelphia, PA: Fortress Press, 1975), 99.

[14] Martin Luther, *Luther's Works* Vol. 40, 88.

[15] Sergiusz Michalski, *Reformation and the Visual Arts* (London: Routledge, 1993), 72.

[16] John Calvin, *Institutes of the Christian Religion*, Book 1, chapter 11, section 5.

[17] Leslie P. Spelman, "Calvin and the Arts," *The Journal of Aesthetics and Art Criticism* 6, no. 3 (1948): 250.

[18] John Calvin, *Institutes of the Christian Religion*, Book 1, chapter 11, section 12.

[19] John Calvin, *Opera Omnia* Vol. 26, eds. Edouard Cunitz and Johann-Wilhelm Baum (Braunschweig-Berlin: C.A.Schwetschke and Son, 1863), 150–151. When considering the validity of Calvin's remarks, it is important to note that the *essence* of God is quite different from the *presence* of God.

[20] Charles Garside, *Zwingli and the Arts* (New Haven, CT: Yale University Press, 1966), 156. For Bullinger, see Andrew Morrall,

"The Family at Table: Protestant Identity, Self-Representation and the Limits of the Visual in Seventeenth-Century Zurich," *Art History*, 40 no. 2 (April 2017), 340.

Chapter 4 Here, There, Everywhere (and Ever-Where)

[1] Augustine, *Confessions*, 6.4.

[2] George Orwell's Big Brother is a totalitarian leader who wields oppressive power for the sake of power, not for the sake of the citizenry.

[3] Karl Rahner, "Lent," in *The Eternal Year*, 68.

[4] Karl Rahner, "Before God," in *Prayers for a Lifetime* (New York: Crossroad, 1984), 4.

[5] If you think I'm just making up a show with a ridiculous name, I invite you to listen to the Janis Joplin song, *Mercedes Benz* (it's on her posthumous 1971 album, *Pearl*). In the second verse Joplin name-checks *Dialing for Dollars*. You can now use this fun fact to win lucrative *Dialing for Dollars*-sized wagers with your friends.

[6] Karl Rahner, "Christmas: The Answer of Silence," in *Everyday Faith* (New York: Herder, 1967), 25.

[7] Augustine, *Tractates on the Gospel According to John* (*In Johannis evangelium tractatus*) 2.10.

[8] Forty-two years after the Beatles split, I had a "favourite Beatle" discussion with a teenage girl in a theatre queue while waiting to see the motion picture *Yellow Submarine*. The poor misguided youth had fallen under the spell of "the cute one." Sadly, her mother was accompanying her, but failed to nudge her daughter towards the correct answer (which again, is George).

[9] For a refresher on "pre-apprehension" see pages 21-22. See also, Williams, *Graced Existence* (Burnaby, BC: Gabriel and Ives Academic, 2020), 19-28.

[10] Karl Rahner, "Ash Wednesday," in *The Eternal Year*, 60.

[11] Augustine, *Confessions* 1.1.

[12] If you want to tickle your brain at the source, check out Socrates working through "Meno's paradox" in Plato's *Meno*. Your local public library will have a copy (or it will shamefully lose all claims to library legitimacy).

[13] Karl Rahner, "Opening," in *Prayers for a Lifetime*, 3.

Chapter 5 Mystery (or Discussing a Place Beyond Words)

[1] Good for you for flipping to the notes section to fact check my Paul mystery claim! The following verses give an overview of the ways in which Paul used *mystērion* (μυστήριον for those conversant in Greek) in his letters:
Romans 16:25; 1 Corinthians 2:1, 7; 4:1; 13:2; 14:2; 15:51;
Ephesians 1:9; 3:3, 4, 9; 5:3; 6:19; Colossians 1:26, 27; 2:2; 4:3;
2 Thessalonians 2:7; 1 Timothy 3:9, 16.

[2] Peter Lombard, *Sentences* Book 4, Distinction 1, Part 1, 4.

[3] Yes, this statement is a bit like dipping our toes into the shallow end of God's enormous pool of grace. Yes again, grace deserves a bigger splash on our part. Hang out poolside and we'll do a full-blown cannonball into the deep end in chapter seven.

[4] If you would like a second historical opinion on the co-mingling of sign and signified, here's some insight from the learned French priest, Alger of Liége (ca. 1055-1132): "A sacrament and a mystery differ in this respect that sacrament is a visible sign signifying some-thing, while a mystery is something hidden that it signifies. However, one can be used for the other ... with the consequence that a mystery is both concealing and concealed, and a sacrament is both signifying and signified." *De Sacramentis Corporis et Sanguine Domini* 1, c.5. Alger of Liége's quote appears in Henri de Lubac, *Corpus Mysticum* (Notre Dame, IN: University of Notre Dame Press, 2007), 49.

[5] Thomas Aquinas, *Summa Contra Gentiles* 1, chapters 30, 29, and 33), *Summa Theologica* I, q. 4, art. 3.

6 Karl Rahner, "Christmas: Grace in the Human Abyss," in *Everyday Faith*, 39.

7 Karl Rahner, "The Answer to Silence," in *Everyday Faith*, 24.

8 This quote is from Rahner's essay, *The Concept of Mystery in Catholic Theology* (in *Theological Investigations* Vol. 4, 59). It echoes the (apophatic) theological approach of Dionysius the Aereopagite (ca. 500, also referred to as Pseudo Dionysius or Denys), who has been a significant influence in the Eastern Church. The idea that God surpasses all that we can fathom also has deep roots in Western theological tradition. Augustine wrote that "compared with [God's] knowledge, our knowledge is ignorance" (*Confessions* 11.6). In the same vein, Anselm of Canterbury (ca. 1033-1109) lovingly conceded: "O Lord, thou art not only that than which a greater cannot be conceived, but thou art a being greater than can be conceived" (*Proslogium* 15).

9 Karl Rahner, "Science as a Confession," in *Theological Investigations* Vol. 3, 395.

10 A tip of the genealogical hat to the memory of Elizabeth Wells (1825-1873) and Joseph Williams (1826-1882). Their marriage (ca. 1857) made my present allusion to coattail literary legitimacy possible. One hundred and sixty-three years is a particularly long set-up time for a footnote. Many thanks to all involved for their foresight.

11 Augustine, *Confessions* 11.17.

12 Thankfully Augustine does not let his understanding of human limitation prevent him from beating his head against the wall of eternal mystery: "My mind is on fire to solve this incredibly complicated conundrum." (*Confessions* 11.28).

13 Although time and human history are two different things, they come together when Jesus simultaneously exists in both (as *Logos* and human being). Human history is the history of God's continuous self-offer, and thus also exists in relation to eternity. Jesus, God's fullest revelation in history, manifestly reveals the eternal God in human history. In this way God, who being eternal

is outside of time, enters time to literally flesh out God's self-offer. Jesus is fully and eternally God, but also fully human in human history. The resurrection of Jesus following his crucifixion and death joins all humanity to God, and brings the human experience of time to eternity. Jesus' participation in time as we know it, means that there is a sacramental aspect to time. Time is another facet of our sacramental orientation – something akin to a sacramental location in which we find our selves. All time ultimately refers to God. Time, points human *being* to the mystery of God's eternal being.

[14] This is key: Even though eternity is outside of time, time exists in relation to eternity.

Chapter 6 Secular Stuff (and Sacred Space)

[1] Jerry Park and Joseph Baker, "What Would Jesus Buy: American Consumption of Religious and Spiritual Material Goods," *Journal for the Scientific Study of Religion* 46, no. 4 (December 2007): 501.

[2] Charles Brown, "Selling Faith: Marketing Christian Popular Culture to Christian and Non-Christian Audiences," *Journal of Religion and Popular Culture, 24,* no.1 (Spring 2012): 120.

[3] Colleen McDannell, *Material Christianity: Religion and Popular Culture in America* (New Haven: Yale University Press, 1995), 259.

[4] Founded as The Christian Booksellers Association, it came to be known simply as CBA.

[5] Colleen McDannell, *Material Christianity: Religion and Popular Culture in America*, 1995), 222. (Note that "over 7000 locations" is a combined estimate of CBA members and non-member retailers).

[6] Charles Brown, "Selling Faith", 113.

[7] Curious readers will find this marketing fact and the aforementioned 300,000 products here:
christianbook.com/page/info/company-history?event=about-us/1008971 (accessed November 7, 2020).

[8] If you spend more time on your computer than your phone, you

can decorate it with a "Coffee Gets Me Started, Jesus Keeps Me Going" decal. Of course, if you're at home in the Eastern Orthodox Church you may prefer a "Jesus Christ golden icon MacBook sleeve." Sorry … I really, really wish that these weren't real products.

9 Skye Jethani, *The Divine Commodity: Discovering a Faith Beyond Consumer Christianity* (Grand Rapids, MI: Zondervan, 2009), 19.

10 Yes, this is a real slogan used by the Late for the Sky Production Company, makers of Bibleopoly, to lure you in. They're also promoting Shark-opoly, which they claim "is gonna be JAWESOME!" If that isn't for you, there is always Geek-opoly or Zombie-opoly, or Rodeo-opoly or … well, you get the idea.

11 It takes some fancy interpreting of the *Constitution of the United States of America* to get around this "enshrined secularity" point. As the White House website states: "The First Amendment provides that Congress make no law respecting an establishment of religion or prohibiting its free exercise." This officially ratified hands-off religion (no promotion / no suppression) statement is a textbook definition of secularism. You'll find this quote (which I accessed on January 2, 2021) here:
www.whitehouse.gov/about-the-white-house/the-constitution/

12 Rahner, "Fear of the Spirit," in *The Great Church Year*, 216.

13 Don't let this "Summer of '69" reference fool you into thinking that Bryan Adams was also "just the right age." Adams was born in 1959, and was too old in 1969 to legitimately challenge my (totally unsuspicious) *last-of-the-boomers* claim.

Chapter 7 Grace (of God, Agents, and Otters)

1 Railroad enthusiasts are serious about accuracy, so I'll clarify a few things about Grace station. It was originally constructed as part of the privately owned Northwestern Elevated Railroad. Grace became part of the Chicago Elevated Railways Collateral Trust in 1913, which morphed into the Chicago Rapid Transit

Company in 1924. The Chicago Transit Authority acquired the station in 1947.

[2] Popeye actually said "I yam what I yam and dats all what I yam." He had little concern for the Queen's English, but made up for it by convincing youngsters to eat a superfood (spinach) long before the term "superfood" entered the nutritionists' lexicon. Incidentally, I am aware of the irony of using Popeye's "I am" to illustrate a point about the grace of "I Am Who I Am" (*'ehyeh 'ăšer 'ehyeh*). A quick review of Exodus 3:13 will reveal that "I Am" is the kind of answer you get if you ask God, "What is your name?"

[3] This has a dark side. If a person is a low-life confidence trickster trying to fool someone, that is (sadly) also part of their being.

[4] The relationship between grace and experience features in *Graced Existence*, my academic companion book to the (considerably funnier) book you're holding. If you would like to dig deeper into the overlap of grace and experience in everyday life, and the theology of Karl Rahner in general, give it a whirl. Randy Mark Williams, *Graced Existence: Grace and Experience in the Theology of Karl Rahner* (Gabriel and Ives Editions, 2020).

[5] Karl Rahner and Wilhelm Thüsing, *A New Christology* (New York: Seabury Press, 1980), 16.

[6] Ingolf Dalferth, "Representing God's Presence," *International Journal of Systematic Theology* 3, no. 3 (November 2001), 241.

Chapter 8 Hope (in God, Neighbour, and Ink)

[1] I sourced this weighty estimate straight from the masters of Doh: playdoh.hasbro.com/en-ca/faq (accessed August 3, 2020).

[2] Yes, there really is a National Toy Hall of Fame. It is located in Rochester, New York. Other inductees into the Hall include traditional toys like alphabet blocks, the bicycle, and the cardboard box! Among branded toys there are enduring favourites like Raggedy-Ann and Andy, LEGO, Etch A Sketch, Silly Putty,

and the Easy Bake Oven. Visit them here: toyhalloffame.org/toys (accessed August 3, 2020).

[3] Karl Rahner, "Easter and Hope," in *The Great Church Year*, 188.

[4] Karl Rahner, "Easter and Hope," 188.

[5] Karl Rahner, "Easter and Hope," 187.

[6] Augustine, *On Faith, Hope, and Love (Enchiridion)* 2.8.

[7] For another account of this see Matthew 22:37-40.

[8] Karl Rahner, "What if There Were Nothing More to Do?," in *Biblical Homilies*, 110.

[9] Augustine, *On Faith, Hope, and Love (Enchiridion)* 2.8.

[10] Karl Rahner and Wilhelm Thüsing, *A New Christology*, 17.

[11] Karl Rahner, *Everyday Faith*, 114.

[12] Karl Rahner, *Everyday Faith*, 114.

[13] Karl Rahner, *Everyday Faith*, 71.

[14] The words recorded in Luke 4:18 reiterate Isaiah 61:1-2 and Isaiah 58:6.

[15] Jimmy Carter, *A Full Life: Reflections at Ninety* (New York: Simon & Schuster, 2015), 95. Carter also shared this story in his book *Living Faith*, and remarked on it during a Sunday School lesson he taught at Maranatha Baptist Church in Plains, Georgia. This can be heard on the audio book *Sunday Mornings in Plains Vol. II: Measuring our Success - Bible Study with Jimmy Carter* (Simon & Schuster Audio, 2007).

[16] Karl Rahner "Love of God and Those Furthest Away," in *The Great Church Year*, 266.

[17] It has taken eight chapters but I've finally squeezed in two separate and unique Sylvester Stallone references. That's not too shabby for a book attempting to impart theological insights.

[18] If you're a fan of municipal bylaw documents, you can peruse it here: hope.ca/file/483. I accessed this on October 12, 2020.

[19] Karl Rahner, "If the Heart is Alive it Thinks of God," in *Biblical Homilies*, 151.

[20] Karl Rahner, "What if There Were Nothing More to Do?," 112.

Chapter 9 Love (in Neon and Whispers)

[1] Cereologists take their name from Ceres, the Roman goddess of agriculture.

[2] All Harlequin Romance books are required to have a "happily ever after" ending. Fun fact: if each of the 6.8 *Billion* Harlequin books sold between 1949 and 2020 have had an average length of 221 pages, we can credit Harlequin with pumping out over 1.5 *Trillion* pages of flirtatious fiction. Yes, that's a lot of love-longing, beckoning firemen, and enfolding embraces. No, I don't blame you for wanting to fact check this. Visit their corporate love nest here: corporate.harlequin.com/

[3] This Pew Research Center survey was conducted from October 16 to October 28, 2019. It involved a nationally representative survey of 4,860 adults in the United States.
For the single-and-curious among us, you'll find more details (including online dating success rates) here:
pewresearch.org/internet/2020/02/06/the-virtues-and-downsides-of-online-dating/

[4] Karl Rahner, *The Eternal Yes* (Denville, NJ: Dimension Books, 1970), 12.

[5] Hériménil is located three hundred and fifty kilometers east of Paris. For readers who missed the metric trip to Hope and are still mileage motoring in Grace, Idaho, that is about 217 miles.

[6] You can find English translations of Lawrence's *The Practice of the Presence of God* for free online in the excellent Christian Classics Ethereal Library collection (ccel.org). If you don't mind spending a few bob, the Critical Edition of *Practicing the Presence of God* from ICS Publications has a terrific translation by Salvatore Sciurba, and excellent biographical material. The following Lawrence quotations are from Sciurba's translation.

[7] Lawrence, *Writings and Conversations on the Practice of the Presence of God*, ed. Conrad De Meester (Washington: ICS Publications, 1994), 97.

[8] Lawrence, *Writings and Conversations on the Practice of the Presence of God*, 38.

[9] Lawrence, *Writings and Conversations on the Practice of the Presence of God*, 42-43.

[10] Lawrence,*Writings and Conversations on the Practice of the Presence of God*, 45.

[11] Lawrence,*Writings and Conversations on the Practice of the Presence of God*, 58.

[12] Lawrence,*Writings and Conversations on the Practice of the Presence of God*, 107.

[13] Ignatius Loyola, "Spiritual Journal," in *Woodstock Letters* 87, no. 3 (July 1958): 226.

[14] Ignatius Loyola, "Letter to Father Anotonio Bradão (June 1, 1551)," in *Letters of St. Ignatius Loyola*, trans. William Young (Chicago: Loyola University Press, 1959), 240.

Chapter 10   Walk On (and Fill in the Blanks)

[1] Yes, I know that Phileas Fogg travelled by air, but even the cranky guys at the back of the NUV refuse to argue that balloons count as "speedy" aeronautics.

[2] Sweepstakes enthusiasts and inquisitive tax accountants take note: In his account Huld wrote that "Phileas Fogg spent 19,000 pounds, about a hundred thousand dollars on his trip. I was less expensive than that … My tickets and all cost about three hundred pounds sterling, about fifteen hundred dollars." Palle Huld, *A Boy Scout Around the World*, trans. Eleanor Hard (New York: Coward-McCann Inc., 1929), 190.

[3] This quote was included in Huld's obituary, as it appeared in the December 14, 2010 print edition of the British newspaper *The Independent*. You can read it yourself, here:
independent.co.uk/news/obituaries/palle-huld-actor-whose-round-the-world-journey-was-the-inspiration-for-lsquotintinrsquo-2159471.html

[4] Yes, there are four ellipses in the last two paragraphs. Get it ... we're pausing ... and slowing down. It's a walking ... noticing ... thing.

[5] Karl Rahner, "Profiting from Every Situation," in *Biblical Homilies*, 58.

[6] Karl Rahner, New Year Meditation," in *Everyday Faith*, 68.

[7] Louis Dupré, "Of Holy Signs," in *Symbols of the Sacred*, 6.

[8] Yes, cat lovers, this is a real video and a really sad commentary on what currently passes for entertainment.

[9] Karl Rahner, "Theos in the New Testament," in *Theological Investigations* Vol. 1, 111.

[10] Covenants are always two-way streets that require both parties to participate and cooperate. For a sampling of what this looks like in scripture, read Genesis 17:1-8; Exodus 19:1-9; 2 Samuel 7:5-16; Jeremiah 31:31-34; and Luke 22:14-20.

[11] Karl Rahner, *The Eternal Yes*, 10-11.

[12] Karl Rahner, "The Great Joy," in *Everyday Faith*, 29.

Praise for *Graced Existence*
the companion volume to
Noticing the Constant Offer of God

"In this clear and carefully researched work, Williams does a remarkable job of contextualizing and unpacking Karl Rahner's contention that grace is the 'ever-present companion of human life.' Far from abstract, Graced Existence is designed to help readers identify and respond to the gift of God's love in their everyday lives."

Nicholas Olkovich
Assistant Professor, Marie Anne Blondin Chair in Catholic Theology
St. Mark's College

"Clearly written and thoroughly researched, this work will be stimulating to Rahner specialists and beginners. Williams is expert at locating aspects of Rahner's thought within [his] overarching theology of grace ... Williams engages contemporary reception of Rahner in a manner that clarifies his thought and exhibits the ongoing relevance of his work for engagement with the world."

Richard Topping,
Principal & Professor of Studies in the Reformed Tradition
Vancouver School of Theology

Randy Mark Williams
Graced Existence

Gabriel and Ives Academic
An imprint of *Gabriel and Ives Editions*
ISBN 978-1-7771-78703

Graced Existence

Grace and Experience in the Theology of Karl Rahner

Randy Mark Williams

Manufactured by Amazon.ca
Bolton, ON

32566087R00125